Vaulting Ambition

Vaulting Ambition

FDR's Campaign to Pack the Supreme Court

Michael Nelson

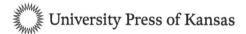
University Press of Kansas

Published by the University Press of Kansas (Lawrence, Kansas 66045), which
was organized by the Kansas Board of Regents and is operated and funded by
Emporia State University, Fort Hays State University, Kansas State University,
Pittsburg State University, the University of Kansas, and Wichita State
University.

Library of Congress Cataloging-in-Publication Data

Names: Nelson, Michael, 1949- author.
Title: Vaulting ambition : FDR's campaign to pack the Supreme Court /
    Michael Nelson.
Description: Lawrence, Kansas : University Press of Kansas, [2023] |
    Series: Landmark Presidential decisions | Includes bibliographical
    references and index.
Identifiers: LCCN 2022055159 (print) | LCCN 2022055160 (ebook)
    ISBN 9780700635351 (cloth)
    ISBN 9780700634125 (paperback)
    ISBN 9780700634132 (ebook)
Subjects: LCSH: United States. Supreme Court—History. | Judges—Selection
    and appointment—United States. | Law—Political aspects—United States.
    | United States—Politics and government—1933-1945.
Classification: LCC KF8742 .N456 2023 (print) | LCC KF8742 (ebook) | DDC
    347.73/26—dc23/eng/20221115
LC record available at https://lccn.loc.gov/2022055159.
LC ebook record available at https://lccn.loc.gov/2022055160.

British Library Cataloguing-in-Publication Data is available.

Printed in the United States of America

10 9 8 7 6 5 4 3 2 1

The paper used in this publication is acid free and meets the minimum
requirements of the American National Standard for Permanence of Paper for
Printed Library Materials Z39.48–1992.

Education is the soul of society as it passes from one generation to another.

G. K. Chesterton

To the educational institutions that have nurtured and sustained me:

New Milford, New Jersey, public schools
The College of William and Mary
The Johns Hopkins University
Vanderbilt University
University of Virginia, Miller Center
Rhodes College

CONTENTS

FOREWORD

When Franklin Roosevelt took the presidential oath of office for the first time in 1933, one governmental symbol was conspicuously absent as he gazed across the east lawn of the Capitol grounds. At the corner of First Street and Maryland Avenue stood the half-completed US Supreme Court building. The institution that Roosevelt would attack after his 1936 reelection did not have a home of its own at the beginning of Roosevelt's first term. Until 1937, the nation's highest tribunal had to make do with courtroom space in the Capitol. The justices had no offices and had to work from home.

Perhaps the absence of a concrete representation of the Supreme Court is among the many reasons Roosevelt miscalculated in his gambit to pack the tribunal. How could the president listed by scholars as one of the three greatest chief executives (along with Washington and Lincoln) make such a glaring error in judgment? Even for those familiar with FDR's court-packing scheme, Professor Michael Nelson's dramatic narrative of the historical details and political machinations makes compelling reading.

The only child of a doting mother, Franklin Roosevelt exhibited supreme confidence throughout his life that even a paralyzing bout with polio in 1921 could not diminish. In addition, his experience as governor of New York, when he procured advisory opinions on proposed policies from the state's high court judges, combined with vast Democratic majorities in both houses of Congress during his presidency, undoubtedly contributed to FDR's inflated sense of self-assurance regarding the federal government's "third branch."

As the scholarly editor of the University Press of Kansas's Landmark Presidential Decisions series and an award-winning author on the presidency, Nelson provides a clear outline of the decision points FDR faced in developing his ill-fated court-packing plan. At every fork in the road, Roosevelt chose the wrong path. His timing, his consultation process, and his misreading of Congress, public opinion, and interest groups were all uncharacteristically off base. His wife Eleanor Roosevelt noted that, once her husband's longtime adviser and friend Louis Howe died in 1936, no one in the president's circle could play the role of unvarnished truth-teller to the chief executive.

Moreover, FDR's Machiavellian propensity toward duplicity to meet his political goals rose to its highest level as he tried to reshape all three branches of government and the Democratic Party in his own New Deal image and likeness. As the British would say, Roosevelt was "too clever by half" in formulating his plan to add a new justice to the Supreme Court for every member over age seventy, up to a full complement of fifteen. His premise that the court was behind in its work because more than half the jurists were septuagenarians failed to convince any constituencies, especially after Chief Justice Charles Evans Hughes reported that the justices were completely up to date on their docket. Both supporters and opponents of the Roosevelt administration knew that the president's animus arose from the court's voiding of more than a dozen New Deal laws in his first term. Yet even ardent New Dealers in Congress and among voters, three-fifths of whom reelected FDR in 1936, supported the Supreme Court's independence as a coequal branch of government. FDR's attempted power grab smacked of authoritarianism just as the United States faced the rise of dictatorships in pre–World War II Europe. Roosevelt would have to pack the tribunal the old-fashioned way, eventually replacing all nine justices one by one as they left the bench.

Among Professor Nelson's unique contributions to the telling of this historic tale are his account of FDR's simultaneous effort to secure congressional authority to dominate the executive branch bureaucracy and his explanation of Justice Owen Roberts's evolution on the court. With regard to the latter, was it less a case of the proverbial "switch in time that saved nine," prompted by FDR's landslide reelection or court-packing threats, and more a response to the justice's failure to obtain the 1936 Republican presidential nomination? More expansively, *Vaulting Ambition* presents an object lesson for second-term presidents, if we ever have another who is reelected by a landslide: hubris truncated Lyndon Johnson's and Richard Nixon's political careers and besmirched FDR's and Ronald Reagan's presidencies.

Barbara A. Perry
Charlottesville, Virginia

PREFACE

Starting in 2005, Republican presidents George W. Bush and Donald J. Trump remade the Supreme Court by filling five vacancies with federal court of appeals judges who had well-established records of judicial conservativism. These justices joined Justice Clarence Thomas, a conservative appointed by Bush's father, to form a six-member majority on a number of significant constitutional issues. Aiding the effort to remake the Supreme Court was a determined faction of the Republican Party and a Senate GOP leader, Mitch McConnell, whose primary focus was the judiciary. In short order, after Justice Antonin Scalia died in February 2016, McConnell persuaded his Republican colleagues to refuse to consider Barack Obama's nominee to replace him, Merrick Garland, because it was a presidential election year. After Trump won the 2016 election, McConnell and the Republican-controlled Senate voted to bar filibusters of Supreme Court nominations and confirm the appointment of Trump nominees Neil Gorsuch in 2017, Brett Kavanaugh in 2018, and Amy Coney Barrett in 2020, even though Barrett's nomination also occurred in an election year.

Democratic activists reacted to this series of events by proposing a number of changes to the Supreme Court. None of these proposals received more attention—including from Joseph Biden, the party's successful presidential candidate in 2020—than the one to increase the number of justices on the court and "pack" it with enough Biden nominees to outvote the existing conservative majority. After becoming president in 2021, Biden appointed the Commission on the Supreme Court to consider various reforms. Two prominent commission members— former federal district judge Nancy Gertner and constitutional law professor Laurence Tribe—argued that "a Supreme Court that has been effectively packed by one party" would benefit from the addition of four justices by the new Democratic president, thereby creating an immediate seven-to-six liberal majority.[1] A bill to expand the number of justices from nine to thirteen was introduced in the Senate by Edward J. Markey of Massachusetts and in the House of Representatives by Jerrold Nadler of New York. Biden's appointment of Kentanji Brown Jackson to replace retiring justice Stephen Breyer in 2022 did little to diminish interest in the idea because it left the conservative majority unaffected. The court's ruling in *Dobbs v. Jackson Women's Health Organization*—with all six Republican-appointed justices in the majority and all three Democrat-appointed justices in the minority—and the controversial decision to overturn its 1973 ruling upholding abortion rights in *Roe v. Wade* provided an additional impetus for advocates of adding justices to the Supreme Court. Prominent progressive Democrats, including Senator Elizabeth Warren of Massachusetts and Representative Alexandria Ocasio-Cortez of New York, immediately renewed the call to expand the court.[2]

Determining the size of the Supreme Court is a matter the Constitution leaves to Congress. Exercising this power, legislators changed the number of justices several times during the first eight decades of the republic. Usually, they did so to accommodate the growing number of states, but not always. In 1801 the outgoing Federalist-dominated Congress reduced the court from six justices to five in an effort to deny an appointment to President Thomas Jefferson, a Democratic-Republican. The ploy did not work: Jefferson and his party's majority in the next Congress restored the number to six. In 1866 the Republican Congress took a similar approach for a similar reason, gradually shrinking the court (which had grown to ten justices) to seven to prevent Democratic president Andrew Johnson from reshaping it. Three years later, with the presidency back in Ulysses S. Grant's safely Republican hands, Congress raised the number of justices to nine, where it has remained ever since.

Germane as these early and mid-nineteenth-century actions may be to twenty-first-century advocates (and opponents) of altering the size of the Supreme Court, considerably more scholarly and public attention has been directed toward the only previous effort to do so in nearly a century: Franklin D. Roosevelt's campaign to add as many as six justices to the Supreme Court in 1937. Then, as in the early 2020s, a liberal Democratic president and Congress were motivated by frustration with a conservative, mostly Republican-appointed court.

Those interested in learning about FDR's court-packing effort have no shortage of works available to enlighten them, ranging chronologically from journalist Joseph Alsop and Turner Catledge's *The 168 Days*

(1938) to attorney Jeff Shesol's *Supreme Power: Franklin Roosevelt vs. the Supreme Court* (2010). To excellent effect, they and other authors, including historians William E. Leuchtenburg and Marian C. McKenna, focus on FDR's plan, the Supreme Court's response, and the plan's rejection by Congress. These and other works on the subject are discussed in this book's bibliographic essay, along with biographies, autobiographies, and oral histories of key players in the controversy; broader works on the Roosevelt presidency; analyses of FDR's campaign for executive branch reorganization; and other related subjects.

This book's approach to the court-packing episode has two additional features. First, unlike most works on the subject, my focus is more on the president's decisions than the court's responses. I say *decisions* because the court-packing effort involved a series of them, including whether to take any action at all.

With this in mind, the book unfolds in narrative form. It begins *in media res* with a prologue describing the State of the Union address Roosevelt delivered to Congress and the country on January 6, 1937, on the eve of his campaign to make the judicial and executive branches more amenable to presidential control. Chapters 1–3 trace the dramatic events that set the stage for this campaign: FDR's rise to power, the ambitious set of New Deal legislative accomplishments that marked his first term, the resistance to these efforts in the Supreme Court, and the president's growing conviction that he and Congress needed to do something to remove the court as an obstacle. Do something—but what? Change the court or change the Constitution? Seek simple legislation or a constitutional amendment?

By the start of his second term, Roosevelt had answered these questions: he would seek legislation (not an amendment) to change the Supreme Court (not the Constitution). Chapters 4 and 5 describe a series of seven decisions he made in the effort to accomplish this goal:

Decision 1: Pack the court—plus

Decision 2: Present the court-packing decision as something other than it was

Decision 3: Take for granted the support of congressional Democrats

Decision 4: Go public with a different justification for the court bill

Decision 5: Attack the justices for acting politically, but underestimate their political savvy

Decision 6: Do not compromise—until it is too late

Decision 7: Sacrifice the executive reorganization bill to campaign for the court bill

Second, while keeping the court-packing effort front and center, I approach it in the context of FDR's larger campaign to embed the New Deal in the major institutions of national government and politics. He strove to do so not just temporarily, with laws passed to meet the crisis of the Great Depression, but lastingly, making changes to Congress, the Democratic Party, and the executive branch, as well as the Supreme Court. In particular, I recount FDR's 1937 campaign, which overlapped the court-packing effort, to secure congressional authority to reform the executive branch bureaucracy in ways that would enhance presidential control. These were understandable efforts. When Roosevelt took office, he inherited a judiciary and a bureaucracy that had been staffed by Republican presidents for twenty-eight of the last thirty-six years, including the previous twelve. Congress, too, had been Republican for most of this period, and the Democratic Party itself was still far from monolithically liberal and therefore not necessarily committed to preserving and extending the New Deal once the Depression was over.

Did Roosevelt succeed? Yes and no. In the final chapter, I assess his uneven record in each of these four institutional domains: the Supreme Court, the executive branch, Congress, and the Democratic Party.

Vaulting Ambition has benefited from the work of many hands. At the University Press of Kansas, I am especially grateful to senior editor David Congdon, managing director Kelly Chrisman Jacques, production editor Erica Nicholson, and freelance copy editor Linda Lotz. Peer reviewers Jeffrey Crouch and Donald Ritchie provided careful and helpful advice, as did friends and colleagues Timothy S. Huebner and W. Taylor Reveley III. Barbara A. Perry, who serves on the advisory board for the Landmark Presidential Decisions series, lent her time, talent, and grace to the book by writing its foreword.

PROLOGUE: JANUARY 6, 1937

At 2:00 P.M. on January 6, 1937, President Franklin D. Roosevelt stood in the chamber of the House of Representatives to deliver the annual State of the Union address to a wildly cheering and deferential Congress. In just two weeks he would be inaugurated for his second and, as he and nearly everyone else presumed, final term.

Here is what the president saw as he surveyed the room: first and foremost, an assemblage of senators and representatives packed with so many fellow Democrats that, of necessity, they spilled over into the traditionally Republican side of the center aisle. He assumed he could depend on their support for his second-term agenda, no matter what he proposed. Many of them had ridden his coattails into office in the 1932 presidential election, the 1934 midterm, his reelection in 1936, or all three. During that time, the party's membership in the House of Representatives had grown from 216 before FDR took office to 333 in the new Seventy-Fifth Congress. The Democrats' Senate caucus had risen from forty-seven to seventy-six members. Compared with all previous Congresses dating back to the Jacksonian era, many more of these Democrats (70 percent of House members and 71 percent of senators) were northerners or westerners. Most of them were FDR-style liberals rather than southern conservatives, although the party's history of southern white conservatism meant that a majority of its House and Senate leaders were from the South. That included both men sitting behind and above Roosevelt during his address, facing the audience: Vice President John Nance Garner of Texas and Speaker of the House William Bankhead of Alabama.

To be sure, even conservative southern Democrats had supported many New Deal measures during Roosevelt's first term, especially relief measures that pumped money into the economies of their disproportionately impoverished constituencies. But southern support in Congress was conditional, requiring concessions designed to keep the region's Black population in subjection—for example, by excluding agricultural and domestic workers, many of whom were African American, from the recently enacted Social Security program. As such, FDR could not count on southern congressional Democrats' support to last, especially now that he had succeeded in bringing previously Republican Black voters into his 1936 reelection coalition, where they reasonably expected the president to make progress on civil rights and other issues in exchange for their endorsement.

No matter, FDR thought. He had already reduced the South's power in Democratic presidential politics by persuading the party's 1936 national convention to abolish its two-thirds rule for nomination, which had long allowed southern Democrats to veto any presidential candidate they found objectionable. Although Roosevelt swept the still solidly Democratic South in both 1932 and 1936, he could have won without a single southern electoral vote, making him the first Democrat since Andrew Jackson to win two terms without needing the South's support. (FDR's most recent Democratic predecessor, Woodrow Wilson, had lost the rest of the country by 155 to 254 electoral votes in 1916, securing his reelection only by carrying the South 122 to 0.) Roosevelt's electoral majority was built on a coalition in which Blacks, liberals, union members, and Catholics and Jews of European descent far outnumbered white southerners. With three-fourths majorities in both chambers of Congress, Roosevelt thought he no longer needed southern Democratic votes to enact his legislative agenda, freeing him to remake the ideologically diverse Democratic Party into the nation's liberal party.

From his vantage point at the podium in the House chamber, Roosevelt could see several executive branch officials in the audience: the secretaries of the ten departments and the heads of several agencies.[1] New agencies had proliferated during the president's first term to such an extent that he no longer had the time, attention, or ability to monitor, coordinate, and direct their activities. Roosevelt's staff in the White House was relatively small and largely clerical—certainly too small to keep up with the growth of the executive branch bureaucracy spawned by the New Deal. As for the government's regulatory agencies—some of them long standing, such as the Interstate Commerce Commission, and others the product of New Deal legislation, such as the Federal Communications Commission—they were designed to be independent of presidential control, further complicating the administrative challenges facing the chief executive. Even subordinate executive agencies were prone to capture by organized groups and congressional barons—the so-called iron triangles.

FDR understood bureaucracy from the inside, having served as assistant secretary of the navy for eight years during the Wilson administration. He confessed that his uneven ability to administer the executive branch had been his main political weakness during his first term, and he was relieved when the Republicans did not exploit that issue in the 1936 election. Now, as part of his second-term agenda, he would correct this failing by asking Congress to pass a law bringing the executive departments and agencies solidly under his control.

Supremely confident, FDR did not doubt his ability to lead the Democratic members of Congress, cabinet officers, and agency heads present for his address. "The challenge we met" during the first term, Roosevelt told the audience gathered in the House chamber and the much larger public audience listening on the radio, was "to restore a large measure of material prosperity . . . by refusing to permit unnecessary disagreements to arise between two of our branches of government"—the president and Congress.[2] During the fabled "hundred days" that began FDR's first term, Congress had responded to his leadership by passing fifteen major pieces of legislation designed for "economic recovery through many kinds of assistance to agriculture, industry, and banking." As that term unfolded, Congress passed additional presidential measures, notably the Social Security Act and the pro-union National Labor Relations Act (Wagner Act). These efforts were aimed less at relief than at reform: "deliberate improvement in the personal opportunity and security of the great mass of our people."

Now, on the eve of his second term, Roosevelt told Congress that he sought "a comprehensive overhauling" of the "administrative machinery" of government for the purpose of "modernizing and improving the Executive Branch." Later that month he submitted a reorganization act that, if passed, would consolidate control of the executive branch in the presidency by, among other things, integrating the government's independent agencies into the cabinet departments and expanding the reach and resources of the White House staff.

Control of his party and of Congress was secure, FDR believed, and once the reorganization bill was enacted, control of the executive branch would be too. The remaining problem—the real one, as far as he was concerned—involved those officials who did not attend his speech. Upsetting recent practice, none of the nine justices of the Supreme Court were present. In the past two years, the court had overturned as unconstitutional several of Roosevelt's favored first-term policies and was eager, he thought, to overturn more.

Although Roosevelt had been preoccupied with what to do about the Supreme Court during the latter half of his first term, he rarely spoke of it in public. In this address, even as his plan of attack on the judicial branch was taking shape behind closed doors, he only alluded to the court. "Means must be found," Roosevelt said, "to adapt our legal form and our judicial interpretation to the actual present national needs of the largest progressive democracy in the modern world." And "because there is little fault to be found with the Constitution, . . . the vital need is . . . an increasingly enlightened view with reference to it."

To be sure, one justice was absent from the president's address due to illness and another made it a practice not to attend presidential speeches. But Roosevelt knew the absence of some of the other justices—perhaps most of them—was a deliberate snub. What he did not notice was that many Democratic legislators resented his growing domination of their party and their branch of government, as well as his assumption that they would support whatever he demanded. Senior Democrats, in particular, felt that Roosevelt treated them like presidential courtiers rather than the legislative barons they believed themselves to be. Because party and committee leadership in Congress was a matter of seniority, the Democratic leaders in both chambers were from the generation preceding FDR's. And because the South was the only solidly Democratic region of the country, most of them were southerners: not just Speaker Bankhead and Vice President Garner but also Senate majority leader Joseph T. Robinson of Arkansas, House majority leader Sam Rayburn of Texas, and House Judiciary Committee chair Hatton Sumners, another Texan.

Nor were southern conservatives the only Democratic members of Congress whose resentment of Roosevelt was growing. By 1937, western progressives were nervously watching Europe, where Adolf Hitler of Germany, Benito Mussolini of Italy, and Joseph Stalin of the Soviet

Union had taken advantage of economic crises to transform strong executive leadership into brutal dictatorships. Senator Burton K. Wheeler of Montana was the farthest thing from a southern conservative—he had been an enthusiastic supporter of Roosevelt's first-term recovery and reform agendas—but he and several other progressive members resented what they saw as the president's effort to dominate the government. However objectionable some of the justices' decisions had been, these progressives considered the Supreme Court a more reliable safeguard of civil liberties than the executive.

As for the executive branch officials present in the House chamber, most (but not all) were FDR appointees. By statutory design, regulatory agencies were headed by bipartisan, multimember commissions. Even the political appointees who headed the departments and agencies had, to some degree, accommodated the organizational norms and procedures prevailing in the institutions they led. The permanent, civil service–based executive workforce on which they relied was accustomed to doing things a certain way and had long-standing relationships with the congressional committees and subcommittees that oversaw their activities. Many civil servants had spent most of their careers working in the less active, more conservative Republican administrations that dominated Washington during the first third of the twentieth century.

On the eve of his second inauguration, the first to take place since the Twentieth Amendment advanced the start of the presidential term from March 4 to January 20, Roosevelt was determined to build on his control of the Democratic Party and his mastery of Congress, both of which he thought he had secured with his triumphs in the last three elections. He planned to instruct Congress and the party to extend his control over the other major institutions of national government: the executive branch and, because of its importance and its resistance, the judiciary. Personal ambition aside, Roosevelt wanted to embed the New Deal and the public philosophy it embodied in the permanent institutions of national government and politics. This would occur, he believed, only if the government acted like a "three-horse team" harnessed together. "The three horses are, of course, the three branches of government—the Congress, the Executive, and the courts," he later argued. "Two of the horses are pulling in unison; the third is not"—but it needed to.[3]

The analogy was not precise. To Roosevelt, the "Executive" meant himself, not the larger executive branch, whose submission he fully expected Congress to authorize. But clearly the Supreme Court was his primary concern, the wild horse that needed to be broken, not the sluggish one that needed to be energized.

Ironically, the "vaulting ambition" that led FDR to exceed what Congress and the country were ready to accept in the way of reform was, in its original formulation in Shakespeare's *Macbeth*, horse-related as well. Macbeth compares such ambition to a rider who vaults so powerfully onto a horse that he "o'erleaps" it and crashes to the ground.[4] Less than a month after delivering his State of the Union address, Roosevelt unveiled his plan to break the two recalcitrant horses—the Supreme Court and the executive branch—and bring them in line without, he hoped, o'erleaping them both.

CHAPTER 1

FDR, the Executive Branch, and the Supreme Court

Relief, Reform, and Resistance

Born in 1882, Franklin D. Roosevelt was strongly influenced by the examples of the two most consequential presidents of his young adulthood: Theodore Roosevelt, his fifth cousin and the uncle of his wife, Eleanor, and Woodrow Wilson, in whose administration FDR served as assistant secretary of the navy. It made no difference to FDR that TR and Wilson despised each other or that they were rival candidates in the 1912 presidential election. He learned from both of them, absorbing ideas and practices that later influenced his own presidential decisions regarding the executive branch and, especially, the Supreme Court.

Although Franklin Roosevelt joined the Harvard Republican Club in 1900, when Theodore Roosevelt was the party's vice-presidential candidate, and voted for TR in the 1904 presidential election, he began his political career as the Democratic candidate for a New York state senate seat in 1910. He became a Democrat partly to avoid a potential political rivalry with Theodore Roosevelt's four Republican sons and partly because there was no reason not to: the early twentieth-century Republican and Democratic Parties were more philosophically alike than different, and each had substantial progressive and conservative wings. The extent to which both parties crossed class lines was apparent even as late as 1932, when the then-renowned *Literary Digest* poll, which sampled a massive (more than two million) but disproportionately upper-middle-class cohort of car and telephone owners, continued its unbroken streak of accurately predicting the outcome of the presidential election. Four years later, after the parties realigned during FDR's first term, car and telephone owners had become disproportionately Republican and most other groups of voters disproportionately Democratic, causing the *Literary Digest* poll to famously underestimate Roosevelt's win in 1936 by eighteen percentage points.[1]

In no sense did their difference in party affiliation diminish FDR's admiration for TR, on whom he explicitly modeled his political career as early as age twenty-five.[2] Theodore Roosevelt's ascent to the presidency was marked by service as a New York state legislator, assistant secretary of the navy, governor of New York, and candidate for vice president. Franklin Roosevelt hit every one of those marks, as well as broadly adopting TR's progressive orientation toward public policy and his expansive understanding of executive leadership. These beliefs extended to a willingness to challenge courts when they got in the way. In his 1912 third-party presidential campaign, for example, Theodore Roosevelt proposed that voters be allowed to overturn state court decisions that invalidated laws on constitutional grounds.[3]

TR did not win that election; Woodrow Wilson did. Wilson appreciated that Franklin Roosevelt, then a state senator in New York, stood by the Democratic Party's nominee, even against his cousin. He liked the idea of having a Roosevelt in his administration and granted FDR's wish to become assistant secretary of the navy, the second-ranking position in what was then a full-fledged cabinet department. In peacetime, during Wilson's first term, Roosevelt learned about the federal bureaucracy from the inside—its complexity, its reluctance to change established ways of doing things, and its deep connection with members of Congress.[4]

FDR's experience in the Wilson administration was transformed by America's entry into World War I in 1917. The Lever Food and Fuel Act granted the president authority to regulate almost the entire economy. A variety of wartime agencies—the War Industries Board, War Trade Board, War Finance Corporation, and others—were created to implement these controls. Additional grants of far-reaching presidential authority followed, including the Trading with the Enemy Act, Sedition Act, and Espionage Act. Roosevelt's wartime experience fostered an understanding that, in times of crisis, the government—especially the president—should assume extraordinary powers. It also convinced him that crises require every branch of government to unite behind the common cause.[5]

Like TR, FDR was an unusually young vice-presidential nominee. Theodore was forty-two when he was placed on the Republican ticket in 1900; Franklin was thirty-eight when the Democrats chose him in 1920, a year after TR died. Governor James Cox of Ohio, the party's presidential candidate, noted that FDR "met the geographical requirement" as a New Yorker and "bore a well-known name."[6] Although the Democrats lost the election, Roosevelt acquitted himself well, delivering about eight hundred speeches in nearly forty states and making contact with many local party officials. Widely thought to have a bright future in politics, he was struck down by polio in August 1921, just ten months after the election. He spent the next several years working to revive his political career, with indispensable help from Eleanor. In 1928, in a Republican-dominated national election, FDR was elected governor of New York, which at the time was the leading stepping-stone to a major party presidential nomination. In less than half a century, New York governors Grover Cleveland, Charles Evans Hughes, Al Smith, and Theodore Roosevelt had been their party's nominee for president.

When the Depression hit in 1929, Governor Roosevelt embraced the same all-hands-on-deck approach to crises he had experienced during the wartime Wilson administration. Pursuing a number of ambitious new policies to provide economic relief for New Yorkers, Roosevelt placed himself squarely at the helm of the state government. He prevailed on the legislature to enact new measures, including an innovative unemployment insurance act. Equally significant, he brought in the state courts as part of a three-branch governing team. Rather than waiting for judicial rulings on the legality of his policies, he consulted freely with several of the state's high court judges at the drafting stage. As president, FDR wanted to have similar "consultations between the president and the [US Supreme] Court as to remedies for some of the evils of the depression."[7] "I hope that I can have at least in part the same type of delightful relations with the Supreme Court which I have had with the [New York State] Court of Appeals," the president-elect wrote in 1932 to Justice Benjamin Cardozo, who was chief judge of New York's high court when FDR became governor.[8]

The 1932 Empowering Election and the First New Deal

After a successful term as governor, Roosevelt was handily reelected two years later, expanding his one-point margin of victory in 1928 to twenty-four points in 1930. He then sought and won his party's nomination for president, running against Republican incumbent Herbert Hoover in 1932. In that year alone, the nation's gross domestic product fell by 23 percent (after falling 16 percent in 1931 and 12 percent in 1930), and the unemployment rate soared to 25 percent, eight times its pre-Depression level.[9] Although the Democrats were still the nation's minority party and had lost fourteen of eighteen presidential elections since the eve of the Civil War, including the last three, Roosevelt won a classic empowering victory in November.[10] Despite lacking specifics ("Philosophy? I am a Christian and a Democrat—that's all"), FDR's campaign had a strongly change-oriented theme.[11] "We need to correct, by drastic means if necessary, the faults in our economic system," he said about the ambitious approach he planned to take to end the Depression. "It is common sense to take a method and try it. If it fails, admit it frankly and try another. But above all, try something."[12] In terms of specific actions, FDR compared himself to a quarterback who knows "what the next play is going to be" but cannot choose the play after that "until the next play is run off."[13]

Roosevelt won the nationwide popular vote by a margin of 57 percent to 40 percent, the first Democrat to win a popular majority since Franklin Pierce in 1852. His electoral vote majority was even more impressive: 472 to 59—at the time, the largest margin in history against an incumbent president. In the accompanying congressional elections, the Democrats gained ninety seats in the House of Representatives—the most ever for a presidential candidate's party—and turned a one-seat preelection deficit in the Senate into a twenty-five-seat majority. The combination of FDR's change-oriented campaign, his landslide victory, and his long coattails in the congressional elections set the stage for the enactment of important new legislation.[14]

As president, FDR's first major goal was to relieve the economic distress caused by the Depression—as much relief as possible as quickly as possible. He rejected widespread calls from across the political spectrum to become a dictator, even though, at the time, the term lacked the negative connotations that soon became associated with it. In 1933 many conservatives admired the take-charge leadership of Benito Mussolini in Italy and Adolf Hitler in Germany, while some liberals were attracted to the Soviet Union's Joseph Stalin.[15] "You may have no alternative but to assume dictatorial powers," liberal columnist Walter Lippmann advised FDR. Meanwhile, a popular new movie by right-wing newspaper publisher William Randolph Hearst, *Gabriel over the White House*, offered a positive portrayal of a president-turned-dictator in a time of crisis.[16] Three weeks before FDR's March 4, 1933, inauguration, the Republican governor of Kansas, Alfred M. Landon, urged: "Why not give the president the same powers in this bitter peacetime battle as we would give him in time of war?"[17]

Roosevelt rejected the idea of dictatorship as an emergency measure during the campaign. "Perhaps a dictator, by suspending legality, could accomplish a ruthless clean-up," he wrote, "but we do not want dictators in the United States."[18] Even as he expressed his continuing faith in constitutional government, Roosevelt was clear about his intention to address the national emergency as if it were a war, preferably with Congress's close cooperation, but without it if necessary. "In the event that Congress shall fail to take [action]," he said in his inaugural address, "I shall ask the Congress for one remaining instrument to meet the crisis—broad executive power to wage a war against the emergency, as great as the power that would be given to me if we were in fact invaded by a foreign foe." It was one of five allusions to war in the address, a call for president-led, unified government action reminiscent of that which Roosevelt had seen and applauded under Wilson. Concerning the Supreme Court, Roosevelt implicitly urged it to accept that "our Constitution is so simple and practical that it is possible always to meet extraordinary needs by changes in emphasis and arrangement."[19]

Roosevelt's crisis- and election-fueled mastery of Congress became evident during the "hundred days" that lasted from noon on March 9 to 1:00 A.M. on June 15, 1933, and launched the New Deal. As had occurred during World War I, he first sought what amounted to a government takeover of the nation's banks and then of the larger economy. He felt no reluctance to intervene when banks failed and left their depositors bereft. To do so, he invoked the Trading with the Enemy Act, a wartime measure still on the books that, as broadly interpreted, empowered FDR to close the nation's banks the day after he took office. Four days later, on March 9, he introduced the Emergency Banking Act, which marshaled the full resources of the Federal Reserve Board to support the faltering banks and thereby restore public confidence in the financial system.

The Emergency Banking Act was the first in a relentless succession of Roosevelt-sponsored laws rapidly approved by Congress; remarkably, the act passed in less than eight hours. Public support for the measure was rallied by the first of the president's fireside chats on radio. Members of both parties in the House and Senate, led by veterans of the wartime Congress, bent to the president's will during the hundred days. Among the important laws that followed were the National Industrial Recovery Act and the Agricultural Adjustment Act, which together encompassed virtually the entire economy; the Federal Emergency Relief Act; and bills to create the Civilian Conservation Corps and the Tennessee Valley Authority. In all, fifteen major laws were enacted in spring 1933, an average of one per week—the so-called First New Deal. Other legislation, aimed at structural reform rather than immediate relief, followed in 1934, including acts to create the Securities and Exchange Commission and the Federal Communications Commission.

Although Congress's responsiveness to his leadership was gratifying, Roosevelt was mildly frustrated when he assayed Chief Justice Charles Evans Hughes's willingness to involve the Supreme Court in his campaign for economic recovery. As a lawyer who had absorbed the basic tenets of the "legal realism" school that became prominent during the 1920s, FDR took for granted that judges are as much lawmakers as priestly guardians of the law. The closely related "living Constitution" theory that developed at about the same time offered a jurisprudential rationale for courts to adapt their interpretations of the document to changing circumstances.[20] In an offhand comment during his 1932 election campaign, Roosevelt said as much, lumping the Supreme Court with the elected branches by claiming that, "after March 4, 1929, the Republican Party was in complete control of all branches of the Federal Government—the Executive, the Senate, the House of Representatives, and I might add for good measure, the Supreme Court as well." While serving as governor of New York, Hughes himself had said, "The Constitution is what the judges say it is," a widely quoted remark that many considered an aphoristic statement of the legal realism school.[21] As recently as 1928, Hughes gave a living Constitution–style series of lectures, arguing that "the Court has found its fortress in public opinion" and noting that historically it had "suffered severely from self-inflicted wounds" when it got crosswise with the evolving views of the American people.[22]

Having won the 1932 election decisively, and believing that all branches of government should pull together to address the crisis of the Depression, Roosevelt had his associates sound out Hughes and Justice Harlan Fiske Stone about the possibility of re-creating the system he had implemented as governor of New York—that is, consulting with judges informally while a law was being drafted to determine how the court would regard its constitutionality.[23] Roosevelt's oft-expressed view of the branches of government was that it was the job "of all three [to] work together to meet the living generation's expectations of government."[24] "Well, that may be," Hughes reportedly responded, "but this is an independent branch of government."[25] "You see," Roosevelt lamented to a senator, "he wouldn't cooperate."[26] Hughes and Stone were focused on their specific responsibility to decide actual cases and controversies that arose under the Constitution and laws that had already been enacted.[27]

Despite Roosevelt's disappointment with Hughes, he assumed the Supreme Court would defer to him and to Congress, either because it accepted FDR's election as evidence of the altered political environment to which legal realists expected the judiciary to adapt or because judicial retirements would enable him to place like-minded justices on the court. As political scientists Robert Dahl and Richard Funston later showed, the Supreme Court sometimes lags behind new national majorities, especially in periods of partisan realignment, because its tenured members were selected during the previous political era.[28] Still, as of 1933, seventy-five justices had been appointed to the Supreme Court during the Constitution's first 144 years, a historical average of roughly two presidential appointments per four-year term. Six of the nine justices in 1933 were already in their seventies, another reason to expect timely vacancies to occur. As for Hughes, although he felt bound by protocol to withhold the sort of advice Roosevelt sought, he too was a creature of politics. Like Roosevelt, Hughes had been elected governor of New York (in friendly fashion, they usually addressed each other as "Governor"), and he was his party's nominee for president against Wilson in 1916.[29] Part of Hughes's strength as a presidential candidate was that he maintained sufficient ambiguity about his beliefs that Republicans of all stripes—the progressives who followed TR out of the party in the previous election and the conservatives who stuck with incumbent Republican president William Howard Taft—supported him.[30]

The 1934 Elections and the Second New Deal

The 1934 midterm elections further strengthened Roosevelt's hold on Congress and his party, empowering him for a second round of significant legislative action.[31] Historically, the president's party loses seats at midterm; at the time, the average loss since 1906 was forty-two seats in the House of Representatives and five in the Senate. As Election Day neared, Vice President John Nance Garner judged that losing only thirty-seven seats would be a victory, and most doubted the Democrats would do that well. Instead, they gained nine seats in the House (raising the party's ranks from 313 to 322, or 74 percent of the total membership) and ten seats in the Senate (increasing the Democratic majority from 59 to 69, or 72 percent of the membership, plus several progressive allies from various third parties). These results, which *New York Times* columnist Arthur Krock described as "the most overwhelming victory in the history of American politics," enabled Roosevelt to press Congress to enact what scholars have called the Second New Deal, this one aimed at welfare state–like reform rather than straightforward economic relief.[32]

Liberal Democrats from outside the South, whose numbers grew substantially after the 1932 and 1934 elections, were disposed to support a reform agenda that included programs such as the Social Security Act, the National Labor Relations Act, the Public Utility Holding Company Act, and a steeply progressive income tax, all of which became law in 1935. Southern Democrats, who long had filled every Senate seat and nearly every House seat from their region, were largely pro–New Deal because they liked having federal money flow into their impoverished states and districts in the form of jobs, crop subsidies, and electric power.[33] Pleasing them was important because of their seniority-based control of important congressional committees, which gave them leverage to insist, for example, that the Social Security Act and National Labor Relations Act not cover farmworkers, workers in food-processing plants, or maids and other domestic workers, most of whom were Black.[34] Although not a single piece of civil rights legislation was enacted during Roosevelt's presidency, southern Democrats were increasingly wary of what he might try to do, especially now that northern urban liberals accounted for a large part of the party's congressional ranks. They also fretted that some New Deal relief policies that helped Blacks along with whites were disrupting the South's white governing regime and attracting previously Republican northern Black voters into the Democratic Party, diversifying what had historically been an essentially all-white coalition.[35] Although more conservative than Roosevelt, Vice President Garner, a Texan, was exceptionally helpful in keeping his fellow southern Democrats on board. As a former Speaker of the House, Garner had wide congressional connections and deep legislative experience that benefited FDR, who had never served in Congress.

The Limits of Control: The Executive Branch and the Supreme Court

Roosevelt's control of Congress and the Democratic Party was nearly complete during his first years in office. His command of the executive branch bureaucracy and the Supreme Court—the other bastions of power in Washington whose cooperation he needed to embed the New Deal in the enduring structure of national government and politics—was less secure.

As the chief executive, Roosevelt appointed the heads of the ten executive departments, although in some cases he did so with party unity rather than personal preference in mind. Below the cabinet level, however, he faced a bureaucracy filled with civil servants working in departments and agencies that had been led by Republicans for twenty-eight of the past thirty-six years, including the previous twelve years. The great majority of federal employees were formally nonpartisan, but a significant minority had received patronage appointments as reward for their service to the GOP before having their positions "blanketed in" to the permanent civil service, where they enjoyed tenure.[36] Partisanship aside, the bureaucracy FDR inherited was used to working in a less active government in quieter times. Civil servants enjoyed well-established relationships with members of the congressional committees and subcommittees that oversaw their agencies, many of them led by southern conservatives with long seniority. Their work habits and the organizational procedures they followed to do the government's business were imperfectly suited to the rapid expansion of programs emerging from the New Deal.

During Roosevelt's first two years in office, he worked around the existing bureaucracy as much as possible, persuading Congress to create new agencies to oversee many of the new programs it enacted. "Why not establish a new agency to take over the new duty rather than saddle it to an old institution?" he asked.[37] The advantage offered by the New Deal's twenty new "alphabet agencies"—the NRA, CCC, CWA, PWA, and others—was that they were unencumbered by long-standing routines and relationships, free of civil service hiring requirements, and staffed by enthusiastic supporters of the agencies' missions.[38] But as historian Arthur M. Schlesinger Jr. notes, Roosevelt's "addiction to new organizations became a kind of nervous tic."[39] Over time, the sheer number of new agencies, along with the uneven responsiveness of the old ones, fostered an administrative complexity that overwhelmed the president. In an effort to get a handle on things, FDR improvised one patchwork arrangement after another, including a short-lived National Emergency Council consisting of the heads of the new agencies plus the secretaries of agriculture, commerce, and labor. Neither this council nor any of his other four ad hoc efforts at coordination gave Roosevelt control of the executive branch. Clearly, he concluded, something more needed to be done.[40]

As for the Supreme Court, its fixed personnel and structure did not change at all with the Roosevelt presidency. During the 1920s and early 1930s the court's nine justices—a number determined by Congress in 1869, after decades of tinkering both for partisan reasons and to accommodate the growing country—had a fairly liberal record in civil liberties cases.[41] The process of applying the freedoms in the Bill of Rights to the states began in 1925 with *Gitlow v. New York*. Otherwise conservative justices sometimes led the libertarian majority.[42] But the Supreme Court Roosevelt inherited also had an increasingly conservative record on economic issues.[43] Because the New Deal agenda was heavily economic, the latter record was more worrisome to Roosevelt than the former was reassuring.

Especially concerning to FDR was that only three of the nine justices seemed favorably disposed to economic liberalism: Louis D. Brandeis, a Wilson appointee and, approaching his eighties, the oldest justice; Stone, appointed by Calvin Coolidge; and Cardozo, a recent Hoover appointee. They were outnumbered by four conservatives who voted together on most cases and even car-pooled to and from the court: Willis Van Devanter, appointed by Taft; James McReynolds, a Wilson appointee; George Sutherland (who provided the car they rode in), appointed by Warren G. Harding; and Pierce Butler, another Harding appointee. All four were close to the same age, having been born during or within a year of the Civil War. The three liberals, for their part, met at Brandeis's house to compare notes the night before the court's Saturday conferences.[44]

Supreme Court justices in this era were not as predictably liberal or conservative, based on who appointed them, as they would later become.[45] For example, McReynolds, an archconservative, was appointed by Wilson, and Cardozo, a leading liberal, was appointed by Hoover. Still, it is noteworthy that in the half century preceding Roosevelt's election, Republican presidents appointed an average of two justices every three years and Democratic presidents fewer than one every two years. One reason is that, with a single exception, Republican-appointed justices resigned or retired only when Republican presidents were in office—a practice the Democrat-appointed justices did not emulate.[46] Of the five presidents who appointed the justices serving on the Supreme Court in 1933, four were Republicans; Wilson was the only Democrat.

In close cases involving economic issues, the liberal trio needed the votes of both justices who did not fit squarely into either camp—Hughes and Owen Roberts—while the conservatives needed only one.

Hughes, recently appointed chief justice by Hoover, had previously served as an associate justice from 1910 until his presidential run in 1916 and was generally regarded as the most progressive justice on the court at the time. Roberts, another Hoover appointee, was also a popular choice among progressives because of his work as prosecutor of the Republican miscreants in the Harding administration's Teapot Dome scandal.[47] Although political scientist Glendon Schubert has characterized Hughes and Roberts as "Hughberts" because they often voted together, swinging from left to right and back again, 80 percent or more of the Supreme Court's decisions in the early 1930s were unanimous. Hughes functioned with remarkable effectiveness to fulfill the two basic small-group leadership roles usually performed (if at all) by different justices: task leader, seeing that the work of the court moved forward, and social leader, keeping personal conflicts from impeding that work.[48] Still, the number of close cases—measured as five-to-four votes—kept rising, from two each in 1931 and 1932 to eight in 1933 and nine in 1934 (Roosevelt's first two years as president).[49]

Clearly, FDR could not count on the Supreme Court to support his New Deal legislation, but neither could he assume that it would be hostile. Reassuringly, in important cases in 1933 and especially in 1934, Hughes and Roberts often sided with the three liberals to form a five-member majority. In early 1934 they approved a Minnesota measure imposing a mortgage moratorium and a New York measure regulating the price of milk.[50] In his opinion in the milk case, *Nebbia v. New York*, Roberts expansively declared that "the power to promote the general welfare is inherent in government." To be sure, these cases involved state law, not presidential or congressional authority. But taken by themselves, they appeared to signal a favorable disposition toward New Deal–style government intervention in the economy. Also of some comfort to the president was that three of the four conservatives (all but Butler) and only one of the three liberals (Brandeis) was aged seventy or older and thus beyond the era's customary retirement age (and, for that matter, its average life expectancy).

Even so, during Roosevelt's first two years in office, he became increasingly concerned. Because little of his policy agenda had been laid out during the 1932 campaign, some hasty, even sloppy legislative drafting took place during the hundred days.[51] Like the Supreme Court, the lower federal courts were dominated by judges appointed by a generation of Republican presidents—all but 28 percent of them, as Attorney General Homer S. Cummings reported to Roosevelt.[52] From the start, opponents of the New Deal had considerable success in challenging administration policies in the lower courts, including hundreds of injunctions against federal agencies issued by district court judges that purported to apply to the entire country. Administration lawyers were reluctant to move cases up the appellate ladder for fear of triggering more adverse rulings. Some of these lawyers were less than competent, having been appointed to the Justice Department not for their professional ability but as patronage rewards handed out by Cummings (himself a patronage appointee, having served as chair of the Democratic National Committee and FDR's floor manager at the 1932 Democratic Convention).[53] The government's chief litigator before the Supreme Court, Solicitor General James Crawford Biggs, was widely regarded as incompetent but was not replaced by the highly capable Stanley Reed until March 1935. Only then were other capable lawyers brought into the Justice Department from elsewhere in the government, including Robert H. Jackson, Paul Freund, and Charles E. Wyzanski.[54] Chief Justice Hughes in particular attributed much of the Supreme Court's skepticism about the New Deal to incompetent administration lawyering.[55]

FDR's apprehension rose when no justices retired in 1933 or 1934. According to Hughes, both Van Devanter and Sutherland had been ready to step down in 1932 but decided they could not afford to when Congress voted to cap the annual pension for retired government employees at $10,000, effectively cutting justices' pensions in half.[56] "One of the reasons why some of the judges had stayed was that they couldn't live if they went off the bench," said Robert Jackson. Sutherland, for example, was the sole support of half a dozen family members.[57]

Causing Roosevelt even greater immediate distress was a set of cases—the so-called Gold Clause cases—scheduled to be argued before the Supreme Court on January 10–11, 1935.[58] Just three days earlier, in its first case dealing directly with a New Deal measure, the court had ruled eight to one (with only Cardozo in the minority) that a poorly crafted provision of the National Industrial Recovery Act relating to the interstate shipment of illegally produced "hot" oil was unconstitutional.[59] The economic stakes in the Gold Clause cases were much higher. The litigants challenged the constitutionality of New Deal legislation and executive orders voiding every clause in every contract, private or public, that required payment in gold or its equivalent. Because FDR had devalued the dollar upon taking office, as most industrialized countries did during the global Depression, any requirement that debts be paid in compliance with these contracts would immediately raise borrowers' debt by about 70 percent, sending the already beleaguered economy into free fall.

Hughes's unwillingness to consult with the president on the gold measures as they were being drafted made the outcome of the cases uncertain. Roosevelt and other administration officials were convinced that an adverse ruling would be catastrophic. In anticipation of a possible defeat in the Supreme Court, Attorney General Cummings and Secretary of the Interior Harold L. Ickes urged the president to consider asking Congress to increase the number of justices if the ruling went against him.[60] Robert Jackson mentioned a recent article in *Political Science Quarterly* that claimed President Grant had done exactly that to overturn a previous money-related Supreme Court decision.[61] Although Roosevelt did not accept this advice, he quietly prepared a public message of defiance, a combative refusal to comply if the justices ruled against him. Citing his constitutional oath "to protect the people of the United States to best of my ability," he planned to declare: "To stand idly by and to permit the decision of the Supreme Court to be carried through to its logical, inescapable conclusion would so imperil the economic and political security of this nation" that he would refuse to obey it.[62]

CHAPTER 2

To Do or Not to Do?

On February 18, 1935, with President Franklin D. Roosevelt poised to make a speech of defiance on national radio and possibly send a measure to Capitol Hill asking Congress to immediately increase the size of the Supreme Court, Chief Justice Charles Evans Hughes announced the court's decision in the Gold Clause cases. The majority was narrow: liberal justices Louis Brandeis, Benjamin Cardozo, and Harlan Fiske Stone and swing justices Hughes and Owen Roberts ruled for the government, but with reservations. Regarding the redeemability of government bonds in gold, Hughes took pains in his opinion in one of the three cases to lecture Congress and the president that, constitutionally, they cannot "disregard the obligations of the government at [their] discretion." Only because the plaintiff had suffered no damage, Hughes scolded, did the five justices rule in the administration's favor.[1] The four conservatives—James McReynolds, George Sutherland, Willis Van Devanter, and Pierce Butler—not only dissented but did so in apocalyptic terms. A red-faced McReynolds angrily read their joint opinion from the bench. "This is Nero in his worst form," he added extemporaneously. "And as for the Constitution, it does not seem too much to say that it is gone."[2]

As Roosevelt and his aides realized, the court's decision was a reprieve, not an acquittal, for the First New Deal relief legislation enacted during FDR's first two years in office. Nor did it augur well for the more far-reaching Second New Deal reform policies he planned to pursue during the latter half of his term. On March 13–14, 1935, less than a month after handing down its decisions in the Gold Clause cases, the Supreme

Court heard arguments challenging the Railroad Retirement Act of 1933, which required railroad companies and their employees to contribute to a pension fund for retired workers. On May 5 eight of the nine justices voted the same way in *Railroad Retirement Board v. Alton Railroad Co.* as they had in the Gold Clause cases. Brandeis, Cardozo, Hughes, and Stone sided with the government, and Butler, McReynolds, Sutherland, and Van Devanter voted against it. The difference this time was that Roberts detached himself from Hughes and joined the conservatives to strike down the law. More ominously, in his majority opinion, Roberts went beyond the constitutional due process claim on which the case was decided to express a very narrow view of what the federal government is permitted to do to regulate interstate commerce, ruling out compulsory pensions in particular.[3] In doing so, he virtually invited a legal challenge to the Social Security Act that FDR introduced in January 1935 (even with its avowed reliance on the government's constitutional power "to lay and collect taxes") as well as to other New Deal laws, many of which rested on the same expansive interpretation of Congress's authority "to regulate commerce . . . among the several states" as the Railroad Retirement Act did.

FDR's interest in doing something about the Supreme Court—increase the number of justices by statute; propose a constitutional amendment to expand the powers of government; require, whether by amendment or statute, a two-thirds majority of justices to overturn a law passed by Congress; or adopt some other approach—was piqued by the barely positive outcome of the Gold Clause cases and elevated by the adverse railway pension decision. His concern became a matter of urgency when the court handed down its next round of decisions.

Black Monday

On May 27, 1935—instantly dubbed "Black Monday" by New Dealers—the Supreme Court announced three decisions unfavorable to the president. In *Schechter Poultry Corp. v. United States* the court invalidated the National Industrial Recovery Act for going far beyond the constitutional bounds of both the commerce clause and Congress's authority to delegate discretionary authority to the president.[4] In *Louisville Joint Stock Land*

Bank v. Radford it invalidated the 1934 Frazier-Lemke Farm Bankruptcy Act as an unconstitutional "taking" of private property without compensation.[5] And in *Humphrey's Executor v. United States*, the court ruled that FDR's decision to fire a member of an independent regulatory commission for political reasons exceeded the president's legal authority.[6]

These decisions sent Roosevelt and other New Dealers reeling. For one thing, all three were unanimous. The authors of the court's opinions ranged from the conservative Sutherland (*Humphrey's*) to the moderate Hughes (*Schechter*) to the liberal Brandeis (*Louisville Bank*). "Where was Old Isaiah?" Roosevelt despaired upon first hearing of the decisions, referring to Brandeis. "What about Ben Cardozo?"[7] The answer to the first question was delivered to the president by aides Thomas Corcoran and Benjamin Cohen, whom Justice Brandeis had invited to the court's robing room after the decisions were announced. "I want you to go back and tell the president that we're not going to let this government centralize everything," said Brandeis, whose liberalism departed from Roosevelt's when it came to accepting concentrated power of any kind.[8] FDR's reaction to *Humphrey's* was especially bitter. "He had a very strong feeling that decision was a discrimination against him personally," according to administration attorney Robert Jackson.[9] The court's opinion seemed to accuse FDR of willfully flaunting the law, but as he saw it, his decision to fire the recalcitrant commissioner was consistent with the justices' ruling in *Myers v. United States* just nine years before.[10] "I tell you, Mr. President, they mean to destroy us," Attorney General Homer Cummings told Roosevelt. "We will have to find a way to get rid of the present membership of the Supreme Court."[11]

Roosevelt privately agreed that the justices had gone "out of their way to spite him personally" in *Humphrey's*. He also found the lack of retirements from the court "most unusual" but was not ready to take Cummings's suggestion, which the attorney general had made before.[12] Get rid of all nine justices in the unanimous majority or pack the court with ten additional justices who could outvote them—really? Grant Congress additional powers through a constitutional amendment that the Supreme Court would then claim the power to interpret? And what was the point of requiring a two-thirds majority on constitutional matters when the justices had just voted as one in all three cases?

In policy terms, the immediate effect of the Black Monday decisions was modest. The National Recovery Administration had become increasingly unpopular and was already on its last legs; Humphrey had died a year before his case was decided; and the farm bankruptcy act was not even a New Deal initiative. More worrisome to Roosevelt was what might come next, especially as Congress considered his Second New Deal agenda—Social Security, utilities regulation, a progressive income tax, and other reform measures—in spring 1935, just as the court was issuing its adverse decisions. As for what to do, if anything, about the Supreme Court itself, the adverse reaction to Roosevelt's criticism of the justices' "horse-and-buggy definition" of the commerce clause at his post–Black Monday press conference on May 31 persuaded him that this was not the time for an open attack.[13]

Public silence remained FDR's stance for the remainder of 1935 and nearly all of 1936, even as the Supreme Court resumed its assault on the New Deal, albeit in a series of divided, not unanimous, decisions. Previously a tenant in the Capitol, the court began hearing cases in its new "marble temple" across First Street on October 7, 1935, the traditional start of its term on the first Monday in October. (The elevated bench in the massive courtroom was built to accommodate nine chairs.) Three months later, on January 6, 1936, a six-to-three majority that included both Hughes and Roberts overturned the major components of the Agricultural Adjustment Act of 1933, a central New Deal measure.[14] After upholding the Tennessee Valley Authority Act in February, with only McReynolds dissenting, on May 18 the court declared unconstitutional the Bituminous Coal Conservation Act (Guffey Act) of 1935.[15] The vote to overturn was five to four, with only Roberts joining the court's four conservatives. One week later the same narrow majority voided the Municipal Bankruptcy Act of 1934.[16] In all, the Supreme Court declared fifteen acts of Congress unconstitutional during the second half of Roosevelt's first term, including a record seven acts in 1935 and a new record of eight in 1936.[17] Yet FDR's prediction that such rulings would produce "marching farmers and marching miners and marching workingmen" massed in protest did not come true.[18]

The president broke his public silence only once, after the Supreme

Court announced its decision in *Morehead v. New York ex rel Tipaldo* on June 1, 1936.[19] The case involved a minimum wage law for women passed not by the federal government but by the state of New York. Roberts once again parted ways with Hughes and joined the four conservatives to overturn the New York statute. For the first time, a Supreme Court decision provoked immediate outrage across the political spectrum. "This decision and former decisions" make clear, Roosevelt said in a June 2 press conference, that the court has created a "'no man's land' where no government—state or federal—can function." Former president Herbert Hoover and a large majority of Republican newspapers also denounced the decision.[20]

What to Do?

Even as FDR treaded water in public on matters involving the Supreme Court, saying nothing between May 1, 1935, and June 2, 1936, others did not.[21] As he considered how (and whether) to try to resolve his problems with the court, Roosevelt had no shortage of ideas to draw from. The populist and progressive movements of the late nineteenth and early twentieth centuries had made courts a target of reform. As historian William Leuchtenburg notes, FDR began his political career at a time when "the air was loud with cries for the recall of judges and judicial decisions," including from Theodore Roosevelt.[22] In the 1920s and 1930s such proposals were increasingly aimed at the Supreme Court. Indeed, from 1935 to 1937, more "court-curbing" bills were introduced in Congress than in any other three-year (or thirty-five-year) period in history.[23] As in previous eras of intense court-curbing discussions, dissatisfaction with the Supreme Court came from the political left.[24]

A few of the bills introduced in the mid-1930s, including one that interested Vice President John Nance Garner, former FDR aide Raymond Moley, and senators James F. Byrnes of South Carolina and Robert M. La Follette Jr. of Wisconsin, proposed to amend the Constitution to more expansively define Congress's legislative powers concerning business practices and conditions of labor.[25] The Supreme Court's recent rulings seemed to confine interstate commerce to the transportation of goods—physical products—across state lines. If the Constitution was amended in ways that broadened the government's authority, these re- formers thought, surely the court would change its stance toward the New Deal. After all, as Justice Roberts stated in *U.S. v. Butler* (the Ag- ricultural Adjustment Act case), the court's "one duty [is] to lay the article of the Constitution which is invoked beside the statute which is challenged and to decide whether the latter squares with the former."

Most of the ideas floating around Capitol Hill, however, involved changing the Supreme Court, whether through constitutional amend- ments or simple legislation.[26] One proposal that intrigued Roosevelt would have empowered Congress to repass a law the court had declared unconstitutional after an intervening election, at which point the law would "be purged of its unconstitutionality and take effect."[27] (The ver- sion advanced by progressive Democratic senator Burton Wheeler of Montana, which required a two-thirds vote of both houses of Congress for repassage, was less appealing because such a large majority would be harder to achieve.) Another idea, offered by progressive Republican senator George Norris of Nebraska, stipulated that only a unanimous Supreme Court could overturn a law, obscuring the legal meaning of a nonunanimous majority's ruling of unconstitutionality.[28] Senator La Follette wanted to require the Supreme Court to grant presidential re- quests for advisory opinions about proposed laws before they were en- acted, formalizing the informal relationship FDR had sought but been denied. Floyd Olson, a Farmer-Labor Party senator from Minnesota, proposed a ten-year term limit for justices. Progressive Republican Lynn Frazier of North Dakota wanted to abolish judicial review and advocated impeachment of any justice who voted to invalidate an act of Congress. Others wanted to create vacancies on the Supreme Court either by ex- panding its size to eleven (or fifteen) or by mandating that justices retire at age sixty-five (or seventy).[29] Still others wanted to redefine the court's appellate jurisdiction so that it could not rule on certain constitutional issues, something Congress had done only once regarding Reconstruc- tion legislation. It was not always clear which of these proposals (other than changing the number of justices) could be achieved through legis- lation and which would require amending the Constitution.

Not every proposal aimed at altering the Supreme Court's behavior was punitive. Like Roosevelt, Representative Hatton Sumners of Texas believed that aligning the court with the New Deal meant changing its membership. But he was convinced that the only thing standing between Justices Sutherland and Van Devanter and retirement was their fear that Congress might reimpose the pension reduction that had shrunk retired justice Oliver Wendell Holmes's annual pension from $20,000 to $10,000 in 1932. As chair of the House Judiciary Committee, Sumners wanted to guarantee the justices' financial security by allowing them to retire rather than resign, thereby redefining their status as ordinary federal judges whose pensions were actually salaries, which were protected from reduction by Article III, section 1, of the Constitution.[30] Sutherland, Van Devanter, and four other justices would have been eligible immediately.

Even as proposals to influence the Supreme Court by carrot (Sumners) or stick (all the others) were being offered publicly by members of Congress, private discussions were taking place within the White House and the Justice Department. In deciding what approach to take, the first question Roosevelt needed to answer was whether to do something or nothing. If his answer was something, a second question arose: what, specifically, should he do?

The arguments for doing nothing—that is, simply awaiting more rulings that, if favorable, would eliminate the need for action or, if unfavorable, would put the Supreme Court "pretty far out on a limb" and create "a real issue . . . on which we can go to the country"—were substantial.[31] As Roosevelt had found when he offered even mild public criticism of the court, any proposal to interfere with its independence would be controversial at best. In a typical poll from this period, Gallup reported in the fall of 1935 that only 31 percent of voters supported "limiting the power of the Supreme Court to declare acts of Congress unconstitutional," with 53 percent opposed.[32] FDR cautiously floated various ideas in the press, dictating language to journalist George Creel for publication in *Collier's*. For example, he suggested, "the president will have no other alternative than to go to the country with a constitutional amendment." "Fire that as an opening gun," Roosevelt told Creel in August 1935, but it merely popped. "Nothing was more plain than the lack of public interest," Creel rued after the article appeared in the magazine's September 7 issue.[33]

In addition, there was little doubt that the hasty drafting of much First New Deal legislation and the less-than-able written briefs and oral arguments presented to the court by Solicitor General James Crawford Biggs had been problematic. Perhaps the more carefully drafted Second New Deal legislation and the more competent representation offered by Biggs's replacement, Stanley Reed, would result in more favorable rulings, obviating the need for further action. After all, only one or two justices needed to be persuaded to turn adverse five-to-four and six-to-three rulings around. Perhaps, as elections sometimes had in the past, a sweeping reelection victory for the president in 1936 would convince justices that times had changed and they should adapt. Or perhaps, after a four-year hiatus in judicial retirements and deaths, vacancies would occur in the natural way. "Father Time, with his scythe, is on your side," Senate Judiciary Committee chair Henry Ashurst of Arizona counseled the president.[34]

However reasonable a strategy it may have been, doing nothing was not Roosevelt's natural inclination. "Above all, try something" was his watchword from the 1932 campaign and the hundred days. FDR had convinced himself that a majority of justices were determined to sink him and his administration; he groused to the cabinet that "he expected Mr. Justice McReynolds to still be on the Court when he was a hundred and five years old."[35] To rely on the administration's improved legal advocacy or to wait for retirements—or even encourage them by focusing on Sumners's pension bill—seemed pointless to Roosevelt, especially with the constitutionality of major legislation from the Second New Deal at risk.

But doing something meant doing something in particular. Deciding what that should be posed a threefold challenge. First, how wide a net should the president cast when seeking advice and ideas? FDR's usual practice on legislative and other policy matters was to consult multiple individuals within his administration, as well as members of Congress, trusted journalists and scholars, and others outside government. He relied on this competitive approach to guarantee that he considered an issue from every angle before making a decision.[36] But because changing the Supreme Court or the Constitution was so politically sensitive, Roosevelt kept his circle of advisers small and secret. The risk of this approach was that, not having been widely vetted, his chosen course of action might be unpopular in Congress and the country.

Roosevelt's second challenge was timing: whatever approach he adopted, it had to be launched at a politically opportune moment. The president's strong bias for action was tempered by patience concerning when to act. In late January 1936 FDR ordered his administration to appeal cases to the Supreme Court as rapidly as possible, on the theory that a series of unpopular adverse rulings would rouse public support for court reform. "He is willing to go to the country on this issue," Secretary of the Interior Harold Ickes recorded, "but he wants the issue to be as strong and clear as possible, which means that he hopes the Supreme Court will declare unconstitutional every New Deal case that comes before it."[37] Complicating matters when the country did not respond to the court's decisions as angrily as Roosevelt had predicted was the impending presidential election in November 1936. FDR wanted to run on his first-term record, not on proposals involving the Supreme Court or the Constitution. In all his campaigns for office, FDR focused more on winning the election than on educating the public about the agenda he intended to pursue if he won.

The third and most important challenge facing the president was choosing the right proposal, a job he largely delegated to a small group in the Justice Department. Former National Recovery Administration counsel Donald Richberg was brought in as well.[38] What had been a desultory pace within the department ramped up after the Supreme Court ended its term on June 1 with *Tipaldo* and the opening of the Democratic National Convention loomed on June 23. Although Attorney General Cummings widened the net of consultation on the party's platform to include a few outside scholars—notably, political scientist Edward S. Corwin of Princeton University and William Draper Lewis of the American Law Institute—no consensus emerged.[39] As discussed in chapter 3, the platform language was anodyne, mentioning only the possibility of some sort of "clarifying amendment" to the Constitution.

Throughout 1935, Roosevelt had seemed to think that whatever approach he took would involve a constitutional amendment.[40] Among the proposals being discussed were various amendments to broaden the government's constitutional powers, to make it harder for the Supreme

Court to overturn a law with less than a supermajority of justices, or to make it easier for Congress to overturn a court ruling by reenacting a law after an intervening election.

By early 1936 FDR was growing disillusioned with the amendment approach as too time-consuming and too easily thwarted by special interests manipulating state legislatures during the ratification process. With little correction from Cummings, he overlooked the speed with which the five most recent amendments had been added to the Constitution, starting with the Seventeenth Amendment in 1913. None had taken longer to ratify than the Nineteenth Amendment, which granted women the right to vote (fourteen months). Ratification of the most recent amendment, the Twenty-First, repealing Prohibition, took only nine months. As a way around potentially resistant state legislatures, Congress had entrusted ratification of the repeal amendment to conventions in each state—an option Roosevelt and Cummings seemingly ignored. When it came to amending the Constitution, FDR was hung up on the proposed child labor amendment, which had cleared Congress in 1924 and, more than a decade later, was still languishing in the states.

Roosevelt was on firm ground when it came to constitutional amendments aimed at extending the powers of government. The Supreme Court had ruled against the New Deal on various grounds, including the commerce clause in Article I, the excess delegation of congressional authority to the president (also Article I), the "take care" clause in Article II, the due process clauses in Article V and the Fourteenth Amendment, the equal protection and privileges and immunities clauses (also in the Fourteenth), and the Tenth Amendment. Thus, one could fairly wonder how many amendments it would take, even if the wording was so clear that the justices could not misapply it. Besides, Roosevelt thought, redefining the government's powers by adding expansive new language to the Constitution would concede that the Supreme Court had been correctly interpreting the document as it stood.

Although FDR abandoned the amendment approach to expanding the substantive powers of the federal government no later than early 1936, he was not yet ready to reject procedural amendments relating to the Supreme Court's composition and authority. On January 20 he received a letter from Cummings arguing that "the real difficulty is not with the Constitution but with the judges who interpret it." Cummings recommended "giving serious thought to an amendment to the Constitution (should we find we are forced to that point) which would require the retirement of all federal judges or, at least, all Supreme Court judges, who have reached or who hereafter reach the age of seventy years."[41] Also in the mix of ideas were amendments requiring the agreement of seven (or all nine) justices to overturn a law or allowing Congress to overturn a judicial decision by repassing the law in question.

Agreeing with Cummings that the real problem was the justices, not the Constitution, Roosevelt was soon ready to abandon the amendment approach entirely. For example, soon after he received Cummings's recommendation, he mused to Ickes, why not simply ask Congress whether he should obey each judicial ruling of unconstitutionality, and if Congress "should declare that its own mandate was to be followed," then "ignore the Court."[42] Although Roosevelt quickly saw that outright defiance of a Supreme Court decision might take him a bridge too far politically, his comment shows in what direction his thinking was headed.

Increasing the number of justices on the Supreme Court, which could be done by a simple act of Congress, did not immediately rise to the top of Roosevelt's list, even after he turned away from the constitutional amendment approach. Still, he occasionally took out the idea and toyed with it. In February 1935 FDR considered including court expansion in his planned response to an adverse ruling in the Gold Clause cases, which remained unspoken when the court's decision was favorable. In November he ruminated aloud to the cabinet (and to others) about British prime minister David Lloyd George's threat to increase the size of the House of Lords if it kept obstructing legislation passed by the House of Commons—a threat that led the lords to acquiesce. Still, Roosevelt found the idea of packing the Supreme Court "distasteful."[43]

Roosevelt did not oppose the Sumners plan to guarantee retired justices' compensation, but he did not embrace it either, despite rampant rumors that at least two conservatives, Sutherland and Van Devanter, would retire as soon as their pensions were secured. Roosevelt feared that assuring the justices' financial security would be a time-wasting distraction and was not convinced that it would have the intended effect. Ever since the *Humphrey's* decision, which he regarded as personally insulting, FDR was certain that "the reactionary members of the Court had apparently determined to remain on the bench as long as life continued—for the sole purpose of blocking any program of reform."[44] Viscerally, the idea of rewarding their obstructive conduct was unpalatable.

The Decision Not to Decide

FDR's decision not to adopt any of these specific proposals in 1935–1936 was not unreasonable, even as the Supreme Court continued to issue adverse rulings throughout the spring of 1936. To be sure, he overstated the difficulty of amending the Constitution by underestimating the likelihood that the heavily Democratic Congress would move quickly to provide the two-thirds majority required to approve any amendment and that three-fourths of state conventions would ratify it. But even so, going this route would have taken time, probably allowing the Supreme Court to rule on other important New Deal legislation, such as the Social Security Act and the National Labor Relations Act. As for adding justices or declaring that the president and Congress could jointly overturn an adverse Supreme Court decision, either approach would have been highly controversial. Guaranteeing the justices' retirement income, Roosevelt thought, would be a futile gesture.

Thus, for all the thought FDR gave the matter and all the legwork done in private by Cummings and other administration lawyers, no solution emerged that clearly seemed best. Added to this was the risk that any such proposal would color the president's reelection campaign, which he was determined to run on his first-term record. An April 1936 poll highlighted the risk. Of those who expressed an opinion on the matter, about twice as many Americans agreed that the Supreme Court "has protected the people against rash legislation" as thought the court has "stood in the way of the people's will."[45]

FDR's decision not to decide what to do about the Supreme Court made sense because he had not decided when to do it either. This was a vital question, especially on the eve of the 1936 election.

CHAPTER 3

The 1936 Election

FDR Decides Not to Decide

Franklin D. Roosevelt was determined to embed the New Deal enduringly in the basic institutions of national politics and government: Congress, the courts, the executive branch bureaucracy, and his political party. He began his 1936 reelection campaign seemingly in solid control of the Democratic Party, which he had elevated to majority status for the first time since before the Civil War. With his party's strong majorities in the House of Representatives and the Senate, earned in 1932 and elevated in the 1934 midterms, he also appeared to be in firm control of Congress, which repeatedly passed FDR-sponsored laws during his first three years in office.

In truth, there were cracks in Roosevelt's control of both these institutions. The South was still the most Democratic region of the country but was hardly the most committed to the New Deal's reform agenda. This became increasingly clear as disenfranchised southern Blacks began to benefit from some of FDR's relief programs and enfranchised northern Blacks, along with Jews, ethnic Catholics, union workers, urban dwellers, and liberals—all of them alien to most white southern Democrats—emerged as significant forces within the party.[1] And although the South was increasingly outnumbered in national Democratic circles, in Washington southerners retained their hold on most leadership positions in both congressional chambers.

As for the other centers of power in Washington, the Supreme Court comprised the same nine justices at the end of FDR's first term as it had at the beginning. The executive branch bureaucracy had been transformed by the addition of multiple New Deal agencies, but it still remained outside FDR's complete control. When he first took office, the executive branch was a staid assemblage of established, slow-paced departments and agencies shaped by years of Republican governance and ill-suited to fulfill the new president's programmatic ambitions. By 1936 it was an organizational crazy quilt. Although the myriad new agencies were disposed to follow Roosevelt's lead, they constituted such a congeries of varied and numerous units that they defied presidential coordination.

Roosevelt's main strategic decision regarding his bid for a second term in 1936 was whether to run a retrospective or a prospective campaign. A retrospective campaign would ask the voters to reelect him on the basis of his first-term record. A prospective campaign would ask them to choose his vision for the next four years over that of his Republican rival. Among other things, FDR's decision about the nature of his campaign would have clear implications for what, if anything, he chose to say about the Supreme Court and the executive bureaucracy. Focusing on his first-term record would mean not much talking about his plans for future reforms. Focusing on his plans for a second term would mean talking about them in some detail. A prospective campaign would be higher risk, but it would also reap greater rewards if Roosevelt won in another landslide. Such a victory would give him the right to claim a clear mandate for the reforms he chose to highlight.

The decision was not easy. FDR admitted that his main political vulnerability was his first-term leadership of the executive branch. If he were the Republican candidate running against him, Roosevelt said, "I would say, 'I am for social security, work relief, etc. etc. But the Democrats cannot be trusted with the administration of these fine ideals.' I would cite chapter and verse on WPA [Works Progress Administration] inefficiency—and there's plenty of it."[2] If the Republicans chose to exploit this weakness, not talking about his plans to reform the executive bureaucracy could cost him support. As for the Supreme Court, several administration advisers and some members of Congress, including Senator George Norris, strongly counseled that if Roosevelt intended to do anything about it, he needed to put the issue before the voters.[3] After the January 24, 1936, cabinet meeting, Secretary of the Interior Harold

Ickes had the strong impression that the president "believes the Court will find itself pretty far out on a limb before it is through and that a real issue will be joined on which we can go to the country."[4] William Denman, an old Roosevelt friend and recent appointee to the Ninth Circuit Court of Appeals, urged the president to make judicial reform an issue in the campaign, although Denman's main concern was the backlog of cases in the lower courts. "Your election is certain," he wrote in April, "but the hell of opposition in the next four years is just as certain."[5] In general, recalled speechwriter Samuel I. Rosenman, "not a week went by that didn't bring with it at least one suggestion by some responsible person as to what ought to be done about the Court."[6]

The Executive Branch

FDR's election-year strategy concerning reform of the executive branch was to inoculate himself against any potential charges of inattention to his administrative responsibilities by appointing an expert committee to recommend a course of action. This was not just good politics; it also was good government. As a former governor and former subcabinet official in Woodrow Wilson's Navy Department, Roosevelt had a richer understanding of executive governance than any other president. Most of his predecessors' efforts at executive reorganization had focused on reducing government spending by making the bureaucracy more efficient. Entering 1936, that was also the concern of many members of Congress, led by Democratic senator Harry F. Byrd of Virginia, who chaired the newly formed Select Committee to Investigate the Executive Agencies of the Government, and Democratic representative James Buchanan of Texas, who chaired the House Select Committee on Government Organization.

In contrast, Roosevelt believed that "the true purpose of reorganization was improved management, which would make administration more responsive" to his direction.[7] He commissioned public administration scholar Louis Brownlow, along with fellow scholars Charles E. Merriam and Luther Gulick, to study possible executive branch reforms. But first, Roosevelt got Brownlow to agree that "the primary object of the study should be to discover and invent ways and means to give the president effective managerial direction and control over all departments and agencies of the executive branch."[8] On March 20, 1936, soon after the Senate created the economy-focused Byrd Committee, Roosevelt sent each of the three scholars a letter appointing them to the new President's Committee on Administrative Management. Having acknowledged the issue and set the wheels in motion to address it, FDR maintained a studied silence until the Brownlow Committee submitted its report, which intentionally was scheduled to arrive after the election.[9]

The Supreme Court

Throughout 1936 Roosevelt publicly approached Supreme Court reform in roughly the same way he approached executive branch reform: by seldom talking about it. Unlike his near silence on the bureaucracy, which passed largely unremarked during the campaign, his near silence about the court spoke volumes.

Roosevelt did not consider appointing a Brownlow Committee–style group of legal experts to study the Supreme Court and recommend reforms. Nor, fearing leaks, did he consult individuals within the administration, Congress, or his network of informal advisers as widely as he normally did before making important decisions. With the April 1936 death of Louis Howe, Roosevelt's longtime political right hand, he lost his most reliable source of unvarnished in-house criticism, and no one took Howe's place. According to Eleanor Roosevelt, the result was that "after Louis's death Franklin frequently made his decisions without canvassing all sides of a question."[10] To be sure, Roosevelt still had the Justice Department, as well as a small number of trusted scholars in law schools and political science departments with whom he could consult informally. Not having decided on even a broad strategy for Supreme Court reform, however, and awaiting additional rulings by the justices that might alter the trajectory of events (the court's annual terms ended in late spring), he had good reason to keep his options open well into the election year.

Even more important, as 1936 began, Roosevelt did not count on his own popularity to win reelection. Nor was it certain that in a head-on confrontation with the justices, the Supreme Court's popular standing would be low enough and the president's high enough for him to prevail.

An Uncertain Election

Unimaginable as it might seem in light of Roosevelt's massive landslide victory in November 1936, it was not clear to him or anyone else at the start of the year that he would win. Only nine of his thirty-one predecessors—just two of them Democrats—had won a second consecutive term. Conservative Democrats, including the party's two most recent presidential nominees—former New York governor Al Smith in 1928 and attorney John W. Davis in 1924—bitterly opposed his election. Republicans, having done well in the few elections that took place in 1935 and noting the president's sagging popularity in early 1936, were optimistic. In announcing his candidacy for president in January, Kansas governor Alfred Landon, a progressive Republican and the only GOP governor to be reelected in 1934, described himself not as an archconservative but as a "constitutional liberal." Landon claimed to be uninterested in "condemning everything the opposition party does," even as he criticized the New Deal's "maladministration," the very issue on which FDR felt most vulnerable.[11]

Roosevelt thought he would win, but not easily. On January 30 he estimated he would carry the Electoral College by 325 to 206.[12] Not all his advisers were that optimistic. In July Ickes wrote, "If this campaign is run much longer as it is being run, there will be little chance of defeating Landon. . . . We are losing ground every day."[13] Independent observers were yet more pessimistic about the president's chances. Even counting FDR's victory in 1932, the GOP had won three of the four most recent presidential elections, all of them by landslides. "The Republican Party will poll a far larger popular and electoral vote than in 1932," wrote *New York Times* columnist Arthur Krock in mid-September.[14] Throughout the year, the *Literary Digest* poll, which had accurately predicted every presidential election since its launch in 1916, showed Landon with a clear lead on election eve: 57 percent of the major-party popular vote and 370 electoral votes. The Gallup and Roper polls, created only the year before, lacked the *Digest*'s track record of success and were therefore less widely trusted, but they turned out to be much more accurate. Based on a cross section of the national electorate, both showed FDR narrowly ahead during the summer.[15] But as late as mid-August, even Gallup had Roosevelt in front by only 49 percent to 45 percent, with the challenger leading in nineteen states with 249 electoral votes.[16]

Conservative Supreme Court justices were among those convinced that the voters might reject Roosevelt in 1936. According to his law clerk, James McReynolds was a faithful reader of the *Literary Digest* and took comfort from its predictions: with "Landon gaining, I think we may be due for a change."[17] Willis Van Devanter privately observed on Election Day that Landon had a strong chance of winning.[18] As the Supreme Court continued to issue anti–New Deal rulings during the first half of the year, the conservative justices saw little reason to think the public was siding with the president over them.

Among the justices who took particular interest in the election was Owen Roberts. As early as 1935, columnist Walter Lippmann reported "considerable interest in the idea of going to the Supreme Court for the Republican candidate in 1936. The idea is that Mr. Justice Roberts, having decided against New Deal measures, is to run as the savior of the Constitution." Another prominent columnist, Drew Pearson, made a private note at the time that "Mr. Roberts had eye on Rep[ublican] nomination" and, along with his writing partner Robert Allen, described the justice as having "a bad dose of presidentialitis."[19] Shortly before the Republican National Convention, the *New York Times* predicted that Roberts would receive substantial support from the delegation representing his home state of Pennsylvania.[20] Based on his reputation as prosecutor in the Teapot Dome scandal, Roberts had already been a long-shot possibility at the 1928 and 1932 Republican Conventions. In 1936 he said nothing to discourage interest in his candidacy. Eighteen years later, testifying before a congressional committee, Roberts commented on justices who "have had in the back of their minds a possibility that they might get the nomination for president." In his own case, Roberts recalled, "enthusiastic friends" urged him "to let my name go up as a candidate" while he was on the court. "Of course, I turned a hard face on that thing," he added unpersuasively. "I never had the notion in my mind."[21]

Nearly a century later, the prospect of a Supreme Court justice either emerging from or entering the arena of presidential politics seems far-fetched. But Roberts served in an era when the Supreme Court was—as it had been since the early republic—one of several plausible stepping-stones to the presidency. By one count, nearly one-fourth of the justices appointed to the court during the nineteenth century either contemplated running for president or were considered by others for a presidential candidacy.[22] In 1848, for example, Justice Levi Woodbury was a leading contender for the Whig Party nomination and Justice John McClean for the Democratic nomination. When the Democrats instead chose Lewis Cass, McClean then became a possible Free Soil Party candidate. Legal historian John Frank examined the justice's papers and concluded "there was no day between his appointment to the Court in 1829 and his death in 1860 in which McClean was not aspiring to be someone's choice at the next presidential election."[23] Salmon P. Chase had ambitions for the presidency both before and during his tenure as chief justice. Chase was "possessed," wrote Senator Carl Schurz of Missouri, of the belief "that he owed it to his country and that the country owed it to him that he should be President."[24] More recently, Charles Evans Hughes left the bench in 1916 to become the Republican nominee for president. Other twentieth-century justices—including Hugo Black and especially William O. Douglas—had presidential ambitions while serving on the Supreme Court that lasted well into the 1940s.[25]

Heightening Roberts's prospects in 1936 was that the GOP's pool of plausible candidates from the political arena was much smaller than usual, having been stripped down to only twenty-two senators and eight governors after the massive Republican defeats in 1932 and 1934. And among the Supreme Court's conservatives, only Roberts, who turned fifty-six in 1936, was young enough to be considered. Until the Republican National Convention began on June 9, he had reason to think he had a decent chance of being nominated.

June 9, as it happened, was eight days after Roberts voted with the four conservative justices to overturn the New York law guaranteeing a minimum wage for female workers. If he thought this decision would remind the Republican delegates that he was on their side, he grievously miscalculated. The court's ruling in *Morehead v. New York ex rel. Tipaldo* was the only one that united Republicans with Democrats, conservatives with liberals, in disapproval. Former president Herbert Hoover, an ardent opponent of the New Deal, called for a constitutional amendment restoring to the states "the power they thought they already had" to enact social legislation.[26] All but a handful of Republican newspapers criticized the Supreme Court's decision.[27]

Roberts faced reality: any hope he may have had that his recent conservative rulings would endear him to Republican kingmakers was now forlorn. Not even a deadlocked GOP convention would turn to him after *Tipaldo*. Instead, the delegates nominated Governor Landon, who pledged that if the Supreme Court kept declaring state minimum wage legislation unconstitutional, his party would seek a constitutional amendment that explicitly empowered states to enact such laws.[28]

Many of the Democrats who assembled for their own national convention less than two weeks later were eager not to be outflanked on the left by Landon's promise. On the eve of the convention, Attorney General Homer Cummings reported to Roosevelt on the "growing conviction amongst our friends" that the Democratic platform "should contain some affirmative statement dealing with a constitutional amendment."[29] The raucous response to Kentucky senator Alben Barkley's keynote address confirmed Cummings's report. "Is the Supreme Court beyond reproach?" Barkley asked the delegates. "No," they shouted. "May it be regarded as too sacred to disagree with?" Another loud chorus of noes.[30]

Roosevelt was not persuaded. He was well aware that in recent decades presidential candidates who criticized the courts had suffered for it, including Theodore Roosevelt in 1912. Democratic senator Burton Wheeler, who was Robert M. La Follette Sr.'s vice-presidential running mate on the Progressive Party ticket in 1924, reminded FDR that their platform had included a proposal to allow Congress to overturn Supreme Court decisions, and it "had been used devastatingly against us from one end of the country to the other."[31] Wheeler warned the president that to raise this issue in the 1936 campaign would cost him votes.[32] Roosevelt authorized his party's platform drafters to say only that, when it came to problems afflicting the country that "overflow state boundaries, . . . if these problems cannot be effectively solved by legislation within the Constitution, we will seek such clarifying amendments" as are necessary to do so.[33] The plank was so restrained (even a proposed mention of FDR's "no man's land" reaction to *Tipaldo* was left out) that it placed Democrats to the right of Landon on the matter.[34] And although the platform read precisely as Roosevelt wanted it to, the reference to "legislation within the Constitution" seemed to imply that the Supreme Court had been interpreting the existing document accurately. Nor did Roosevelt mention or even allude to the court in his nationally broadcast speech accepting his party's nomination.

FDR was equally silent about plans for executive branch reform. As with the court, the platform did not mention the subject. Among the four centers of institutional power Roosevelt sought to control—the Supreme Court, the executive bureaucracy, Congress, and the Democratic Party—only the party was targeted at the convention. For decades, southern Democrats held a de facto veto over presidential nominees because the party required a two-thirds majority for nomination. Southern conservatives could not impose a candidate on the party, but they could usually keep anyone they considered unacceptable from being chosen. Roosevelt flexed his political muscles at the 1936 convention and had the two-thirds rule repealed. His plans to make the Democrats the nation's liberal party by empowering his coalition of northern, urban, ethnic, and working-class voters to choose presidential candidates would no longer be impeded by southern resistance.

As for his reelection strategy, "there's one issue in this campaign," Roosevelt told aide Raymond Moley on convention eve: "It's myself."[35] He would conduct his campaign retrospectively as a referendum on his first-term performance. The theme of FDR's opening campaign speech on September 29 and of the dozens that followed was the contrast between "four years ago and now."[36] The result of his first-term initiatives, Roosevelt declared, was that "starvation was averted, that homes and farms were saved, that banks were reopened, that industry revived, and that the dangerous forces subversive of our form of government were turned aside."[37] National income had risen by 50 percent since he took office, while unemployment dropped by more than a third. Business and farm incomes had grown dramatically, and the nation's banking system was saved from collapse.[38]

Roosevelt's strategy soon produced results. During the summer, his campaign had been in the doldrums. An extensive Gallup poll conducted in early July showed that although he had a three-point lead over Landon in the national popular vote, Roosevelt's weakness in the large industrial states of the Northeast and Midwest had him trailing in the Electoral College.[39] These results confirmed similar findings in a private Democratic Party poll.[40] Once Roosevelt started campaigning, however, his support rose to clear majority status.

Determined to call out the president on the issues of the Supreme Court and the Constitution, Landon challenged him directly in an October 29 speech at New York's Madison Square Garden. "What are the president's intentions with respect to the Constitution?" Landon asked. "Does he believe changes are required? If so, will an amendment be submitted to the people or will he attempt to get around the Constitution by tampering with the Supreme Court?" Knowing that FDR was scheduled to speak in the same arena two nights later, Landon dared the president: "Tell us where you stand."[41]

Roosevelt's October 31 speech at the Garden became famous for its fighting rhetoric. "I should like to have it said of my first administration," he roared, "that in it the forces of selfishness and of lust for power met their match. I should like to have it said of my second administration that in it these forces met their master." Yet even in this speech, as in all his previous campaign oratory, Roosevelt's recurring refrain was retrospective: "We will continue." He said nothing about the court. Indeed, other than his June 2 comment about *Tipaldo*, Roosevelt "did not mention the Court even once" all year.[42]

Late in the campaign, Roosevelt confidently calculated that he would be reelected by 360 electoral votes to 171. Maine, which voted in September, went Republican, but by a smaller margin than in 1932, boding well for FDR's national prospects. But even he was astonished by the magnitude of the actual results: a forty-six-state, 523-to-8 victory in the Electoral College and a 61 percent to 37 percent majority in the national popular vote. By gaining six seats, Senate Democrats outnumbered Republicans seventy-six to sixteen in the new Seventy-Fifth Congress, along with four independent progressives. Democrats also added twelve seats in the House, raising their majority to 331 to 89, with 13 independents. By historian James T. Patterson's calculation, only eighteen Senate Democrats and about thirty House Democrats were conservatives, giving liberal Democrats clear majority status in their party's caucuses and in both congressional chambers.[43] At the state level, thirty-three legislatures were controlled by Democrats after the election, compared with only six Republican legislatures.[44]

Roosevelt's personal landslide and long coattails in the congressional contests were hallmarks of his 1932 empowering election victory, which set the stage for major legislative reforms during his first term. The results in 1936 demonstrated that a partisan realignment had occurred. Previously independent or Republican voters who had simply opposed Hoover or supported FDR in 1932 had become Democrats, elevating the party to enduring majority status for the first time in eighty years.[45] Young voters entered the electorate as FDR Democrats.[46] What was missing in 1936 was a change-oriented campaign theme like the one marking Roosevelt's first election. By focusing voters' attention on the previous four years (the "New Deal record") rather than the next four years (the "New Deal promises"), Roosevelt denied himself the mandate he needed to take on the Supreme Court or even the executive bureaucracy.[47] As historian Kenneth S. Davis writes, if Roosevelt had "devote[d] at least one major campaign address to possible ways of overcoming Court obstructionism," he could have claimed "a mandate to move against Court intransigence."[48] But he made no such speech, leaving Ickes to rue that "the groundwork has not been laid" in Congress or the country for enacting a successful program of judicial reform.[49]

Yet in terms of his personal approach to the Supreme Court, the groundwork *was* being laid. As Roosevelt later recalled, "during the summer and fall of 1936," his "studies" of what to do about the court "began to assume a definite shape."[50] Justice Department lawyer Warner W. Gardner reported that in September or October Cummings asked him to compile a report listing and evaluating every possible reform initiative.[51] Clearly, Roosevelt had not yet decided what to do about the Supreme Court, but it is clear that he decided to do something rather than nothing. Although Solicitor General Stanley Reed and Assistant Attorney General Robert Jackson advised him that the justices' attitudes might change as a result of the election, Roosevelt did not believe his landslide victory would lead Hughes and Roberts to adapt their views to the new political reality.[52] Nor did he believe that any of the four conservatives would retire even though their hopes of being replaced by a newly elected Republican president had been dashed. Van Devanter and George Sutherland had wanted to step down for four years. Perhaps enacting the bill to guarantee their pensions would give them a graceful way out.

Not sure what he intended to propose, but not wanting to hand the Republicans an issue in the midst of an election that appeared to be close, Roosevelt was wise not to offer any specific proposals during the campaign. But once he knew that he intended to do something and was confident he would win, the president was unwise not to signal, at least in general terms, his broad intention.

"Wait until next year," Roosevelt told Secretary of the Treasury Henry Morgenthau in May 1936. "I am going to be really radical."[53] But he kept this intention close to the vest and then overinterpreted his reelection victory as being the equivalent of a blank check for the future rather than an endorsement of what he had already accomplished. Landslide minus agenda does not equal mandate, but FDR thought it did, despite polls showing public resistance to proposals to restrict the Supreme Court.[54] In Roosevelt's mind, recalled speechwriter Samuel Rosenman, his margin of victory alone would determine "the size of the mandate that he got in 1936 to see how far he could go," conflating personal support with policy mandate.[55] Perversely, the president argued after the election that, in policy terms, he had "an absolutely free hand" to do what he wanted *because* he had not made any "campaign promises."[56]

Postelection Planning

With the election over and the Supreme Court and the executive bureaucracy in his sights, Roosevelt focused on formulating the reform proposals he wanted the new Congress to enact. He received the Brownlow Committee's draft report on November 14, less than two weeks after the election. He liked almost all of it, including proposals to create a small White House staff to serve as additional eyes and ears on the bureaucracy; to transfer the Bureau of the Budget and the Civil Service Commission to a new Executive Office of the President; and to consolidate the scattered executive agencies into twelve departments along lines determined by the president. Two of the departments would be new: Public Works and Welfare. The Interior Department would be expanded and renamed the Department of Conservation. When Roosevelt told committee members he also wanted to see the independent regulatory commissions absorbed into the departments, Brownlow and his colleagues revised their report accordingly. The satisfied president was ready to make the report public and send legislation to Congress. He had every expectation that the committee's recommendations would become law.[57]

Meanwhile, work was quietly proceeding on a plan for judicial reform. On November 6, three days after the election, Roosevelt waxed expansively about the Supreme Court at his first postelection cabinet meeting. "I think the president is getting ready to move on that issue," recorded Ickes.[58] Less than two weeks later, FDR boarded a ship for a four-week trip to South America, taking along two thick binders of memos compiled by Cummings on various proposals to amend the Constitution or curb the Supreme Court legislatively. While the president was gone, Cummings corresponded with Professor Edward Corwin at Princeton, who was writing a series of newspaper articles that included a recommendation for mandatory judicial retirement at age seventy. The problem was that, by altering the Constitution's provision that judges serve "during good behavior," this approach would almost certainly require a constitutional amendment. But Corwin also enthusiastically passed along to Cummings a *"most* ingenious" idea sent to him by another political scientist, Arthur Holcombe of Harvard University. "What would you say," Holcombe wrote, "to an act of Congress providing that judges under the age of 70 should always comprise a majority of the Court and giving the president power to make additional appointments to the Court" sufficient to outnumber the older justices?[59] The immediate effect of such a plan would be to authorize the appointment of four new justices who, when added to the court's three youngest members, would outnumber the six justices in their seventies.

At about the same time, in mid-December, Cummings was reminded of an entry in the new history of the Justice Department he had coauthored with Carl McFarland, *Federal Justice,* which was about to be published.[60] It described a 1913 recommendation by then–attorney general James McReynolds that for every federal judge seventy and older who did not retire, the president should appoint an additional judge "who will have precedence over the older one."[61] McReynolds had excluded the Supreme Court from his recommendation, but the principle could easily be extended. The devilish pleasure of attacking the Supreme Court's conservatives through a quarter-century-old suggestion by its most ardently anti–New Deal justice was almost irresistible. Also in mid-December Cummings received Gardner's long memorandum assessing the various reform proposals. Although the memo did not endorse the idea of adding justices to the Supreme Court, it did describe this approach as "the only one which is certainly constitutional and . . . may be done quickly and with a fair assurance of success" through simple legislation.[62] (Gardner also noted the potential need for "nine or ten new justices," considering "the likelihood of antagonizing the present liberal justices to the point where they would retaliate by voting against the constitutionality of legislation.")[63] In addition, Cummings already had in his files a series of letters from Judge Denman complaining that the lower federal courts were chronically backlogged with cases and asking that more district and appellate judgeships be created.

By December 22, Roosevelt was well disposed toward the idea of packing the Supreme Court. He summoned journalist George Creel and instructed him to write in *Collier's*: "The president can *enlarge* the Supreme Court, increasing the number of justices so as to permit the appointment of men in tune with the spirit of the age."[64] The focus on age seemed especially timely, considering that a recent book critical of the court by Drew Pearson and Robert Allen, *The Nine Old Men*, had reached the best-seller lists and launched its title phrase into general circulation.[65] On that same day, Cummings sent word to Roosevelt that he was "bursting with ideas" and had formulated "a plan of substance & approach" that he was eager to share with the president.[66] When the two met the day after Christmas, Cummings found that he was pushing on an open door. The problem was not with the Constitution but with the justices' "reactionary misinterpretation" of the document, he told the president. "Go on, you are going good," Roosevelt replied.[67]

Channeling Judge Denman, Cummings went on to say that the lower federal courts were in desperate need of more judges to handle their heavy caseload and then added: "If the federal judiciary as a whole should grow in numbers, there was no particular reason why the Supreme Court should not grow in numbers as well."[68] Citing another 1913 statement that seventy should be the mandatory retirement age for judges, this one by former president and chief justice William Howard Taft, Cummings suggested that Roosevelt seek authorization from Congress to appoint an additional justice for every current member of the Supreme Court who was older than seventy.[69] Such a law could be quickly enacted and "the whole thing could be over within sixty days," Cummings concluded.[70] Assuming no one retired, Roosevelt could immediately appoint six new justices. "The answer to a maiden's prayer," was Roosevelt's blissful response to Cummings's recommendations.[71] The president could not only remake the Supreme Court in his own image but do so in the nonpolitical guise of a judicial reformer seeking only to increase the federal courts' efficiency.

Unlike the competitive advisory process Roosevelt usually employed to ensure he considered every option before choosing one, he consulted a very small circle of advisers in arriving at his approach to court reform.[72] Even as multiple members of Congress—whose votes FDR would need—were preparing their own proposals to amend the Constitution or enact statutory reforms, he froze them out of the discussion.[73] His party's leaders in Congress, on whom he would rely to corral their colleagues, were left in the dark. So was Vice President Garner and, other than Cummings, the cabinet. Nearly all farm, labor, and liberal group leaders whose active grassroots support Roosevelt counted on were left out as well. White House aides on whom the president had relied during his first term remained unaware of what Cummings and Roosevelt were planning. For example, Thomas Corcoran and Benjamin Cohen worked up a proposal largely on their own—a constitutional amendment that would allow Congress to overturn a Supreme Court decision by a two-thirds vote or, after an intervening election, by a simple majority. But when Cohen showed this and another constitutional amendment to the president in January 1937, Roosevelt dismissed them, having already made up his mind.[74]

This lack of consultation left Roosevelt and Cummings blind to some basic political considerations. First, the constitutional amendment path was politically more feasible than they assumed, an assumption they never questioned in their private discussions. Second, any effort to present their plan to pack the Supreme Court with compliant justices as something other than it was would invite not only ridicule but also charges of deviousness and dishonesty. Third, despite their inclination to support the president, Democratic leaders and members of Congress could not be counted on to enact into law what amounted to a power grab against a Supreme Court that most of their constituents did not regard as illegitimate, even though they disagreed with some of its decisions. This was especially true because Roosevelt had never mentioned, even in general terms, any intention to curb the court during his re-election campaign.

As it turned out, the president's obliviousness of these political considerations would impede passage of the Supreme Court bill, and the narrative of a power-hungry president seeking to trample the Constitution would soon extend to his efforts at executive branch reform as well.

CHAPTER 4

The President Proposes

By most reckonings, on January 6, 1937, the date of Franklin Roosevelt's first State of the Union address after his reelection as president, his campaign to embed the New Deal in the permanent institutions of national government and politics was farther along than ever. He had made the Democrats the nation's majority party and remade it in a mostly liberal form. He had reduced the Republican presence in Congress to 17 percent of the Senate and 21 percent of the House of Representatives. Among the Democratic members of Congress, only a minority—about 25 percent of Democrats in the Senate and 10 percent of those in the House—were conservatives.[1] Regarding the executive branch bureaucracy, the Brownlow Committee's recommendations sat on the president's desk, ready to be translated into legislation. And discussions in the White House would soon crystallize into a wide-ranging judicial reform bill with the Supreme Court at its center.

Roosevelt was advancing his campaign for mastery, but he had not reached his destination. Because seniority still ruled the day in Congress, both chambers were led by southern Democrats, including Speaker of the House William Bankhead of Alabama; House majority leader Sam Rayburn of Texas; House Judiciary Committee chair Hatton Sumners, also of Texas; Senate majority leader Joseph Robinson of Arkansas; and Vice President John Nance Garner, another Texan and, constitutionally, the president of the Senate. Among the cohort of veteran congressional progressives, a growing wariness prevailed about ceding more power to the president than had already been relinquished during his first term.

The Supreme Court still consisted of the same nine justices, and most district and appellate court judges also predated his presidency. At least as important as these political realities was FDR's failure to discuss either executive or judicial reform during his reelection campaign, even in the most general terms. His landslide victory was an endorsement of his first-term reforms, not a mandate for additional ones. Indeed, a Gallup poll taken right after the election found that most voters hoped FDR would move in a "more conservative" direction during his second term (50 percent, including 50 percent of Democrats) rather than a "more liberal" direction (only 15 percent, including just 19 percent of Democrats).[2]

In this generally but not entirely favorable political environment, FDR confidently resolved to translate his command of the Democratic Party and Congress into control of the executive and judicial branches.

The Executive Branch

Roosevelt alluded to the courts in his State of the Union address. "The vital need is not an alteration of our fundamental law," he said, referring to the Constitution, "but an increasingly enlightened view in reference to it," presumably on the part of the Supreme Court. Saluting Congress's first-term record of "refusing to permit unnecessary disagreement to arise between two of our branches of government," he added: "It is not to be assumed that there will be a prolonged failure to bring legislative and judicial action into closer harmony. Means must be found to adapt our legal forms and our judicial interpretation to the actual present national needs."[3]

"Leave the whole thing very general for now," the president had told speechwriter Samuel Rosenman, with reference to the Supreme Court.[4] When it came to the executive branch, however, Roosevelt was explicit. In his first charge to Congress, he declared: "Executive management has reached the point where our administrative machinery needs comprehensive overhauling. I shall, therefore, address the Congress more fully in regard to modernizing and improving the executive branch of the government."[5] Two days later the President's Committee on Administrative Management—the Brownlow Committee—publicly released its recommendations for bureaucratic reform, and four days after that, on January 12, Roosevelt asked Congress to enact them into law.

The unifying themes of the Brownlow Committee's report and its thirty-seven recommendations—"strong executive leadership is essential to democratic government" and "the president needs help" to provide it—became the themes of the bill FDR sent to Congress. To control the myriad departments and agencies of the executive bureaucracy, Roosevelt sought an expanded White House staff; a new Executive Office of the President (EOP) consisting of the Bureau of the Budget, the Civil Service Commission, and other broad managerial units previously housed elsewhere in the executive branch; the integration of all one hundred or so agencies, including independent regulatory commissions, into the twelve (up from ten) departments; and improved financial and accounting practices. None of the president's staff aides, and few in the EOP, would be subject to Senate confirmation.[6]

No member of Congress was consulted during the development of the proposed reorganization act, even though, as Brownlow acknowledged, "the leaders of the legislative branch . . . from the beginning of the government had considered themselves responsible for the control, confinement, bridling, and ultimate determination of the organization of all branches of the government."[7] Indeed, each chamber of Congress had recently created its own select committee on reorganization, one chaired by Senator Harry F. Byrd of Virginia and the other by Representative James Buchanan of Texas, both conservatives. Yet when Roosevelt met with Democratic congressional leaders just two days before sending his bill to Congress, he made it clear that he was informing them, not consulting them. "There will be no exceptions, not one," he told Rayburn, who asked whether the Interstate Commerce Commission could remain independent.[8] Afterward, Roosevelt crowed to Brownlow, "This was quite a little package to give them this afternoon. Every time they recovered from a blow, I socked them with another one."[9]

Nor did Roosevelt consult with his cabinet, the members of his own team who would be most affected by reorganization. The lack of consultation sent at least one department head, Secretary of Agriculture Henry Wallace, into covert opposition to the bill. Wallace was certain that Interior Secretary Harold Ickes would try to increase his own domain at Wallace's expense, with the Forest Service most likely at risk.[10] Even Attorney General Homer Cummings was uncertain about the measure, raising doubts about the constitutionality of its proposed grant of unilateral presidential authority to reshape the departments and agencies.[11]

The initial reaction to FDR's reorganization act was, as political scientist James MacGregor Burns aptly described it, "quiet hostility."[12] Senators and representatives valued their relationships with the executive agencies they supervised as members of congressional committees and subcommittees. The agencies—the Forest Service, the Army Corps of Engineers, the independent regulatory commissions, and others—were similarly content with the committees they dealt with. Special-interest groups representing veterans, doctors, industrial workers, farmers, business owners, and others were comfortable with both the agencies and their committee overseers on Capitol Hill.[13]

Members of Congress also noticed that the reorganization bill would move the Civil Service Commission into the EOP, extending nonpartisan civil service coverage to many thousands of additional positions, thereby allowing FDR to pack the bureaucracy with New Deal loyalists while denying legislators their traditional patronage appointments. Senator Byrd, whom Roosevelt neither consulted in advance nor included in his briefing of congressional leaders, took the reins in opposing the president's measure.[14] His committee's work on reorganization, which was based on an economy-focused report by the Brookings Institution that took issue with many of the Brownlow Committee's recommendations, was concerned with saving money, not increasing presidential power.

Still, there seemed little doubt that the overwhelmingly Democratic Congress would pass FDR's reorganization act "in a month or six weeks," by Ickes's estimate.[15] Then, on February 5, the president introduced his bill to expand the Supreme Court, titled the Reorganization of the Federal Judiciary Act. Executive reorganization was already an irritant to Democratic members of Congress; paired with judicial reorganization, it became known as the "dictator bill." European dictators were at an early peak of unpopularity in the United States, fueled by Italian dictator Benito Mussolini's conquest of Ethiopia, German dictator Adolf Hitler's remilitarization of the Rhineland, and Soviet dictator Joseph Stalin's "Great Purge" of suspected political opponents. The Committee to Uphold Constitutional Government, a well-funded organization founded by newspaper publisher Frank Gannett and Father Charles E. Coughlin, a demagogic radio preacher with a vast audience, roused grassroots opposition to both of Roosevelt's bills by raising the specter of dictatorship. Members of Congress found themselves bombarded with telegrams—ten thousand sent to Senator Robert Wagner of New York alone—concerning a measure that normally would have been ignored by most voters as uninterestingly abstract and technical.

Work on executive reorganization ground to a halt in the Senate when it became mired in the all-consuming battle over court packing. The House made some progress on executive reorganization while it waited for the Senate to complete its work on the court bill. House leaders decided to divide Roosevelt's reorganization act into four separate pieces of legislation. On July 27, by a vote of 260 to 88, it approved a bill authorizing the president to hire six new staff members. After exempting multiple independent regulatory commissions and limiting the president's reorganization power to two years, the House voted 283 to 76 to authorize FDR to regroup existing agencies into departments, including a new Department of Welfare. The other two bills, one dealing with government accounting and auditing and the other with the civil service, did not pass in the House. In August, after the court fight was over, Democratic senator James Byrnes of South Carolina proposed a measure that incorporated the two successful House bills, along with modified versions of the two that failed. But when the House received Byrnes's proposal, it referred it to the chamber's Rules Committee, chaired by anti–New Deal representative John J. O'Connor of New York. Although Roosevelt made executive reorganization the centerpiece of a special session of Congress in November 1937, nothing was enacted.

The Courts

Roosevelt moved from saying nothing about the courts during his reelection campaign to alluding to the need for judicial change in his January 6 State of the Union address to celebrating the Constitutional Convention at his inaugural address two weeks later for its creation of "a strong government with powers of united action." These cautious but steady rhetorical steps were intended to prepare Congress and the American people for judicial reform.[16] Whether his proposal would take the form of a statute or a constitutional amendment, and whether it would aim at altering the powers of government or the powers of the courts within that government, remained to be seen.

Clearly, something was coming, but what? And whatever it was, how would Roosevelt get it enacted? Starting with his choices about what to propose, the president made a series of important decisions, both in anticipation of and in reaction to the responses of Congress, the Supreme Court, the broader political community, and the public. Initially, FDR's decision-making process was internal, focused on what to propose and how to present it. Once his proposal was launched, however, the process became iterative: presidential decision, political reaction, subsequent presidential decision in light of that reaction, and so on. Three of these major decisions and the reactions to them are discussed in this chapter; four others are discussed in chapter 5.

Decision 1: Pack the Court—Plus

From a long menu of possible reforms, Roosevelt decided to ask Congress to pass a law increasing the size of the Supreme Court from nine justices to as many as fifteen, depending on how many of the six justices aged seventy years or older chose to retire. That decision, although not irrevocable, was apparently made during the weeks after the 1936 election, culminating in the president's meeting with Cummings on December 26. Roosevelt then decided to embed his court-packing proposal within a larger framework of reform encompassing the entire federal judiciary.

Deciding on the Supreme Court–related aspects of this approach meant rejecting a number of other possibilities. As discussed in chapter 3, waiting to see whether some conservative justices would either alter their behavior or retire in response to Roosevelt's victory in the 1936 election was unacceptable to him. "Either the election was only a mirage," argued administration lawyer Robert Jackson, counseling patience, "or the Court must yield."[17] But Roosevelt refused to believe that anything would change the justices' minds, despite a pair of pro–New Deal decisions by the Supreme Court in late December 1936 and early January 1937, one unanimous and the other nearly so.[18] Representative Hatton Sumners's bill to encourage retirements by guaranteeing former justices' financial security was not something the president opposed, but neither was it something he thought he could rely on. Proposing one or more constitutional amendments to redefine the powers of government would require faith in the Supreme Court's willingness to not impose its own narrow interpretation on whatever amendments were added—as well as a concession that the justices had been correctly interpreting the existing Constitution. Roosevelt was also concerned that any constitutional amendment—for example, allowing Congress to overturn an adverse Supreme Court decision, establishing a mandatory retirement age for justices, or requiring a two-thirds majority of the court to rule a law unconstitutional—would take too long to work its way through Congress and, especially, the state ratification process, with no guarantee that it would be enacted.

In deciding not to pursue any of these approaches, all of which had supporters in his administration or in Congress, Roosevelt also decided to rely on a single chief adviser, Attorney General Cummings, in determining his course of action. Consulting with other cabinet members or congressional leaders, Roosevelt thought, would invite leaks to the press, "which would tip off the opposition" or, worse, give others a voice in a decision he claimed as his own.[19] Roosevelt did not mind leaks, but only if he did the leaking (as noted in previous chapters, he anonymously floated court-related trial balloons to George Creel of *Collier's* as recently as December 1936). Besides, FDR assumed, congressional Democrats, party leaders around the country, and the myriad labor, farm, and liberal groups that faithfully supported the New Deal would surely follow his lead, wherever he chose to take them.

Consulting almost exclusively with Cummings throughout January 1937, Roosevelt overlooked some obvious considerations. For one, age correlated only imperfectly with judicial resistance to the New Deal. The youngest justice, Owen Roberts, was part of the conservative majority, and the oldest, Louis Brandeis, was in the liberal minority. (Oliver Wendell Holmes, another liberal icon, was ninety when he retired from the court in 1932.) In three of the seven cases that overturned federal New Deal statutes, the vote had been nine to zero or eight to one, which meant that adding six young and reliably pro–New Deal justices would not guarantee a compliant court.[20] Even so, six was an audacious number. The size of the Supreme Court had occasionally been altered in the past, but not since 1869, always in increments of one or two, and almost always at the initiative of Congress, not the president.[21]

Roosevelt "hadn't had anybody look at the scheme as devil's advocate," said Robert Jackson.[22] Underlying FDR's lack of consultation—which differed considerably from his way of doing things during the previous four years—was that he read too much meaning into the results of the 1936 election. He had asked the voters whether they approved of his first-term performance, and they said yes. He did not mention reforming the Supreme Court during the campaign but assumed they would say yes to that as well, despite considerable evidence in public opinion polls that most Americans respected an independent Supreme Court, even when they disagreed with some of its decisions.[23] The Democratic platform merely stated that the president's party might consider seeking "clarifying amendments" to the Constitution.

During the first ten days of Congress's 1937 session, members proposed nearly fifty constitutional amendments, almost none of which involved increasing the size of the Supreme Court. Most were designed to enhance Congress's power to legislate rather than the president's power to appoint.[24] House Speaker Bankhead and Senate majority leader Robinson readied their party caucuses for an amendment campaign focused on broadening the powers of government, keeping in mind the accelerated nine-month pace at which the most recent amendment, Prohibition repeal, was enacted after Congress assigned ratification decisions to state conventions rather than legislatures.[25] Not knowing what Roosevelt had in mind, Senate Judiciary Committee chair Henry Ashurst of Arizona denounced court packing as "the prelude to tyranny" when introducing his own constitutional amendment. Answering Republican charges that packing the court was exactly what Roosevelt planned to do, Ashurst said, "A more ridiculous, absurd and unjust a criticism of a president was never made."[26]

In addition to proposing to increase the number of justices, Roosevelt readily succumbed to the attorney general's suggestion that court packing be presented to Congress and the country as a logical, uncontroversial component of a comprehensive program to make the federal court system more efficient from top to bottom. District and appellate courts had to handle so many cases, Cummings argued, that they were way behind in their work. The solution was to ask Congress to create fifty new lower court judgeships, as well as to authorize the appointment of a system-wide proctor who could untangle knots in the system by moving judges from less busy courts to busier ones. One result of more efficient lower courts would be an increased flow of appeals to the Supreme Court, which, according to Cummings, was also behind in its work. In this context, he concluded, adding more and younger justices to help the older ones handle the increased volume of cases could be considered a nonpartisan, commonsense measure.

At a minimum, deciding on a plan in private rather than consulting more widely denied the president insight into how his proposal might be received, especially by those whose support he would need to pass it. Focusing with Cummings on court reform in isolation from his nearly simultaneous proposal for executive reorganization kept Roosevelt from seeing that, taken together, they might be seen as a dictatorial power grab. Working without consultation also opened the door for other critics of the Supreme Court to become invested in their own approaches to reform, not knowing what the president might recommend. It meant subjecting parts of FDR's recommendation that were not widely vetted for accuracy to factual refutation. Finally, the efficiency rationale for appointing more judges and justices was not only disingenuous but transparently so. No one doubted that Roosevelt's real motive was to alter the partisan and ideological makeup of the court, not to help older, more conservative jurists do their jobs better.

Decision 2: Present the Court-Packing Plan as Something Other Than It Was

On January 30 Roosevelt was satisfied with the basics of his and Cummings's proposal and brought in a few other aides to help refine the three documents he intended to send to Congress: the bill itself, an accompaning message from the president, and a letter from Cummings explaining why the entire federal court system needed to be reformed. The slightly expanded roster of advisers included occasional speechwriter Samuel Rosenman, former administration attorney Donald Richberg, and Solicitor General Stanley Reed.

When these advisers saw what Roosevelt had in mind, they were appalled by both the proposal to pack the Supreme Court and the "appearance of deceptiveness" created by the elaborate apparatus in which court packing was embedded.[27] Reed pointed out that he and Cummings had just sent their annual report to Congress stating that the courts were on top of their work and the Supreme Court in particular would do well to hear fewer cases, not more.[28] Rosenman observed that "it was hard to understand how [FDR] expected to make people believe that he was suddenly interested primarily in delayed justice rather than in ending a tortured interpretation of the Constitution."[29] Dismissing their concerns, Roosevelt informed the group that their job was to refine the language in his message to Congress, not to change its substance. Only one significant issue arose during the drafting: should the number of justices remain at fifteen permanently, or should the court shrink when fewer justices were older than seventy? At Cummings's urging, FDR decided that once the Supreme Court was expanded to fifteen justices, it should remain that size.

Roosevelt was eager to launch his plan as soon as possible, in part to stop the momentum for other proposals on Capitol Hill, where many members of Congress were publicly endorsing approaches of their own that they would be forced to abandon in order to support the president's bill. Hoping for relatively quick passage, Roosevelt also wanted to start appointing new justices before the Supreme Court ruled in upcoming cases concerning the Social Security Act and the National Labor Relations Act. Late on the afternoon of February 4, 1937, without telling them what it was about, FDR sent word to Democratic congressional leaders and his cabinet to meet at the White House the next morning. After briefing them, he would meet the press.

Everything about these meetings on the morning of February 5 revealed Roosevelt at his worst: arrogant, duplicitous, enthralled by his own cleverness, and blind to the limited, retrospective nature of his 1936 victory. He spent only half an hour with the cabinet and congressional leaders, first dismissing the amendment approach several of them had publicly endorsed and reading aloud parts of the message to Congress that would accompany his bill, without inviting comment.[30] He then hurried off to meet the press. Afterward, riding back to the Capitol, Sumners said, "Boys, here's where I cash in my chips."[31] This was a crucial defection. Because Sumners, as chair of the House Judiciary Committee, could bottle up Roosevelt's bill and prevent it from coming to the floor, FDR had to abandon his plan to seek rapid House approval that would create momentum for passage in the Senate.[32] Consequently, the upper chamber, with its filibuster rule and independent-minded senior members, would have first crack at the president's proposal.[33] Shortly after noon, as the bill was being read to the Senate, Vice President Garner stepped down from the presiding officer's chair, approached a group of senators, and, in plain sight of all, held his nose with one hand while giving an energetic thumbs-down with the other.[34]

During his meeting with the White House press corps, Roosevelt mixed a careful reading and explication of his message to Congress with winks, smirks, and comic pauses, signaling how cleverly his proposal would tame the Supreme Court while pretending to be about improving judicial efficiency. He began by stating his "very definite conclusion that there is required the same kind of reorganization of the judiciary as . . . for the executive branch"—as if presidential command of the constitutionally independent judicial branch of government belonged in the same category as increased authority over the president's own administrative domain.[35] "He seemed to be asking the assembled newspapermen to applaud the perfections of his scheme, to note its nicely calculated indirections and praise its effectiveness," wrote journalists Joseph Alsop and Turner Catledge.[36] In reality, his proposal's misplaced focus on the supposed inefficiencies in the federal court system made Roosevelt seem ashamed of his best and truest argument for reform: namely, that the Supreme Court was imperiling the elected branches' efforts to lift the country out of the Depression. Four years later, he conceded, "I made one major mistake when I first presented the plan. I did not place enough emphasis on the real mischief—the kind of decision which, as a studied and continued policy, had been coming down from the Supreme Court."[37]

Roosevelt included Sumners's judicial retirement bill in his proposal, but he could not resist taking a shot at the justices. Because their salaries were small, he said, many "would cling to their posts, in many instances far beyond their years of physical or mental capacity," even "to the very edge of the grave." He paused a beat and added, to gales of laughter, "I am talking about 1869."[38] Sumners promptly reintroduced his bill, both houses passed it later that month, and Roosevelt signed it into law on March 1. Within a year, both justices known to be eager to step down pending congressional assurance of their income, George Sutherland and Willis Van Devanter, retired.

Perhaps because of the popularity of Drew Pearson and Robert Allen's best-selling book *The Nine Old Men*—and the stickiness of the title phrase in public discussions of the Supreme Court—Roosevelt tied age to outdated thinking and general ineptitude in his message to Congress. Calling for "a constant infusion of new blood in the courts," he argued that "a lowered mental or physical vigor leads men to avoid an examination of complicated and changed conditions. Little by little, new facts become blurred through old glasses fitted, as it were, for the needs of another generation." This argument was not likely to appeal to the vice president, the Speaker of the House, the Senate majority leader, or the chairs of the two chambers' judiciary committees, all of whom were in their sixties. Nor could liberal admirers of eighty-year-old Justice Brandeis help but wonder how FDR's argument applied to him. In truth, part of what set the nine justices on the Hughes Court apart from the justices in most other periods of history was that none of them could fairly be accused of mental decrepitude.[39]

As Roosevelt himself later admitted, his decision to present the court-packing bill as something other than what it really was constituted a "serious mistake." Its insincerity was obvious. It rested on factual premises concerning the inefficiency of the Supreme Court and the lower courts that were easily refuted. It was disrespectful of senior members of Congress whose support was needed, both in its failure to create even the illusion of advance consultation and in its contemptuous discussion of age. Even when offhandedly endorsing Sumners's bill, Roosevelt implied that judges who awaited the assurance of financial security before retiring were motivated by greed.

FDR did not doom the court bill with his bad decision about how to present it. He was still a popular president with three-fourths majorities in both houses of Congress. But he dug himself a hole that he would have to climb out of it by making better decisions going forward. "The cleverness, the too much cleverness, appealed to him," was Rosenman's verdict.[40]

Decision 3: Take for Granted the Support of Congressional Democrats

Despite springing it on them cold, Roosevelt was confident that a solid majority of Democrats would support his plan. So was the press. The *New York Times* headline on February 6 was: "Congress Startled, but Expected to Approve." Eighty-six percent of voters in a Gallup poll taken a week later said they expected the plan to pass, even though they were divided, with 43 percent "in favor of President Roosevelt's proposal regarding the Supreme Court" and 47 percent opposed.[41] Senator Carter Glass of Virginia said he would "oppose it with all the strength that remains to me" but did not "imagine for a moment that it will do any good. Why, if the president asked Congress to commit suicide tomorrow, they'd do it."[42] FDR's success in getting all but one of his first-term legislative recommendations passed by Congress gave him and nearly everyone else the impression that he was unbeatable.[43]

Roosevelt's confidence was undiminished even after realizing that by alienating Sumners he had lost his preferred option of first seeking passage in the House, where majority support was secure and the threat of a filibuster did not exist. With varying degrees of enthusiasm, majority leader Robinson, Judiciary Committee chair Ashurst, and Vice President Garner agreed to support the bill in the Senate. Robinson did so with particular energy because, in gratitude for his strong and effective support during the 1935 congressional session, Roosevelt had promised the loyal but generally conservative senator a seat on the Supreme Court when one became available.[44] To be sure, Senator Josiah Bailey of North Carolina and a handful of other conservative southern Democrats, worried that a Supreme Court filled with liberal Roosevelt appointees would challenge racial segregation in the South, were certain to defy the president—but what other Democrat would dare?[45] Roosevelt actually looked forward to seeing the Senate's sixteen Republican members take the lead in opposing the bill because that would allow him to rally the Democrats on a partisan basis. He was especially pleased when former president Herbert Hoover immediately blasted his proposal.[46]

Senate Republican leader Charles McNary of Oregon quickly discovered that, for the first time since the GOP divided into progressive and conservative wings in the early twentieth century, his party was united in opposition to the court bill. Astutely, he persuaded his fellow partisans to keep quiet and not play into Roosevelt's hands. "I am inclined to vote no," Democratic senator Carl Hatch of New Mexico told his Republican colleague Arthur Vandenberg of Michigan. "But you Republicans, and particularly Mr. Hoover, must not make it too hard for me."[47] Vandenberg prevailed on Hoover not to give any more speeches. The former president and other national Republican leaders, including Alfred Landon, Roosevelt's opponent in the 1936 election, reluctantly agreed to "muzzle" themselves. As McNary told his colleagues, we will "let the boys across the aisle do the talking."[48]

Roosevelt was slow to catch on to the Republicans' strategy. Nor, more significantly, did he realize how much opposition was developing among "the boys across the aisle," especially independent progressives and liberals in his own party who had entered the Senate before FDR's presidency and did not owe their political success to him.[49] These pre-New Deal progressives reluctantly accepted Congress's steady loss of authority to the president during Roosevelt's first term but were disinclined to support his new campaign for mastery over the executive bureaucracy and the courts. And, although they disagreed with the Supreme Court's decisions to overturn various New Deal laws, they admired the justices' record of support for civil liberties, most recently its unanimous decision on January 4 to prevent states from violating people's First Amendment right to peaceably assemble.[50]

Chief among the progressive Democrats who surprised Roosevelt with his opposition was Burton Wheeler of Montana, an influential fifteen-year veteran of the Senate. Wheeler had reliably supported the New Deal, even taking the lead in getting the Public Utility Holding Companies Act passed in 1935, and was the first major national figure to endorse Roosevelt for the Democratic presidential nomination in 1932. The senator shared FDR's desire to rein in the conservative Supreme Court, but he wanted Congress to do the reining in, empowered by a constitutional amendment that would enable legislators to overturn adverse judicial rulings. What Wheeler did not want was to accelerate Roosevelt's absorption of power into the presidency, a prospect that the recent conduct of European dictators made all the more frightening. Wheeler and other veteran progressives, such as Hiram Johnson of California and George Norris of Nebraska, shared "a hostility to centralized power, whether corporate or governmental." Beyond that, Wheeler felt disrespected by Roosevelt.[51] "Many of us, instead of coming in on the coattails of the president, helped to nominate him," he complained.[52] "Who does Roosevelt think he is? He used to be just one of the barons. I was the baron of the northwest."[53]

Wheeler not only opposed the court bill; he led the opposition to it, meeting secretly with an informal steering committee of more than a dozen Senate colleagues, nearly all of them Democrats, who agreed to engage in "intensive lobbying of our fellow senators" and then share what they learned every day.[54] The volume of constituent letters and telegrams to Democratic senators concerning the court plan was both enormous and overwhelmingly negative, which encouraged several of them to listen to the arguments Wheeler and his allies were making in private conversations.[55] Polls showed no increase in public support for the plan—if anything, support was declining slightly.[56] The president met with one or two Democrats every day at the White House, without changing any minds. By the end of February, he finally understood just how closely divided the Senate was. Threats and enticements delivered at FDR's request by Democratic National Committee chair James A. Farley to either hold up or speed up patronage appointments, depending on whether a senator was cooperative or not, apparently had little effect or, in some cases, an adverse effect.[57] Roosevelt counted about thirty senators on each side, with the remaining thirty-five or so undecided.[58] Yet when Garner, Robinson, and Ashurst met with him on February 20 to suggest a compromise granting the president two or three new appointments, Roosevelt "laughed in their faces."[59] He resolved to stick to his course and "let the opposition blow itself out."[60]

Roosevelt's assumption that congressional Democrats would readily enact his court bill blinded him to some important political realities. One was that, despite the prevailing belief among Democrats that something had to be done to allow the New Deal to pass constitutional muster, this did not necessarily translate into support for the specific course of action FDR proposed. Many of them had already gone on record as favoring some kind of constitutional amendment and were reluctant to embarrass themselves by changing course in response to presidential pressure. Another reality was that senators were bound to recoil if asked to repeat with a straight face the president's transparently false rationale for the bill—namely, that it was a nonpartisan measure aimed at judicial efficiency rather than a power play against the Supreme Court. Yet another political consideration overlooked by the president was that the Republicans were capable of behaving strategically. By not leading the opposition to the bill, they allowed the debate to unfold as a dispute within the president's own party rather than a partisan clash between Republicans and Democrats. Finally, Roosevelt ignored the compounding effect of his simultaneous efforts to master the Supreme Court and the executive bureaucracy among members of Congress concerned about their own branch's waning power. It surely did not help when Mussolini was quoted as endorsing America's "trend toward Fascism's idea of strong, central authority" or when the Nazi-controlled German press praised Roosevelt's court-packing plan.[61]

By March, Roosevelt decided that, rather than cut his losses and seek a compromise, he would change his strategy. The time had come to appeal directly to the American people with a new message, one that he thought would rally their support and, as a result, win over the undecided senators.

CHAPTER 5

The Senate Disposes

After unveiling his court bill on February 5, 1937, two weeks into his second term, President Franklin D. Roosevelt spent the rest of the month working behind the scenes to rally support in the Senate. For various reasons—the most important being the obvious deception of presenting the measure as a wide-ranging, nonpartisan judicial reform bill rather than an ideological assault on the Supreme Court—that support proved hard to get. Attorney General Homer Cummings urged FDR to stay the course and volunteered to make the public case for passing the bill on the grounds of enhanced judicial efficiency. The bill "is reasonable," Cummings said in a February 14 radio address; "it is moderate."[1] Other close Roosevelt aides, including Benjamin Cohen, Thomas Corcoran, and Robert Jackson—all of whom had been frozen out while the court bill was being developed—told the president he needed to go public himself and make the case for passage based on the bill's true purpose.[2] Persuaded at last, Roosevelt acknowledged to Jackson and Solicitor General Stanley Reed on February 25 that the efficiency argument "is a pretty terrible platform to stand on, isn't it?"[3] But the damage had already been done, and it was severe. As Jackson wrote, "The fighting issues, ready-made for the president, were not seized. There was not a word about the usurpation, the unwarranted interferences with lawful government activities, and the tortured constructions of the Constitution."[4]

Decision 4: Go Public with a Different Justification for the Court Bill

Exactly one week after his meeting with Jackson and Reed, Roosevelt broke his public silence on the court bill with a major address, followed in short order by another, with Cohen and Corcoran assigned lead speechwriting responsibility. The occasion for the March 4 address was already on FDR's calendar: the Democratic Party's Victory Dinner, when local activists would gather in banquet halls around the country to celebrate their triumph in the 1936 elections. The second address, a fireside chat, came five days later, on March 9. Even more important than the decision to speak publicly was Roosevelt's resolve to use those speeches to explain his real purpose in taking on the Supreme Court.

FDR delivered his March 4 speech to a live gathering in Washington, but it was broadcast to 1,263 rallies in forty-three states attended by about half a million fellow Democrats. On March 9 he broadcast the first fireside chat of his second term to the entire country on radio. It was the only fireside chat FDR made for the purpose of rousing grassroots pressure on Congress to enact a specific measure.[5]

Jackson told the president the public did not understand the significance or even the meaning of the administration's efficiency-related arguments concerning judicial matters such as "certiorari denied." He advised that "instead of talking about cases the court did not take, we should talk about the cases that they did take."[6] Finally accepting this advice from Jackson and others, Roosevelt took off the rhetorical gloves in his speech to the Democrats. Perhaps to dispute the recurring charge that he was a would-be dictator, he began by announcing that his "great ambition on January 20, 1941"—that is, after completing his second term—"is to turn over this desk and chair in the White House to my successor." Having forsworn any intention to break the two-term tradition for presidents, he turned directly to the Supreme Court, blasting its decisions to overturn the Agricultural Adjustment Act, the National Industrial Recovery Act, the Railroad Retirement Act, the Guffey Coal Act, and New York's minimum wage law. Properly understood, FDR said in language he dictated to his speechwriters, "the American system of government" is "a three-horse team" that must "pull together" so that "the field . . . *will* . . . *be* . . . *ploughed,*" his head bobbing in emphasis. When one horse—the Supreme Court—"lies down in the traces or plunges off in another direction, the field . . . *will* . . . *not* . . . *be* . . . *ploughed.*"[7] This was the same understanding of the court's proper role that had animated his governorship of New York and his early request for an informal consulting relationship with Chief Justice Charles Evans Hughes.

Roosevelt was no less pointed in his fireside chat. Repeating his litany of adverse Supreme Court decisions and invoking once again the "three-horse team" analogy, he charged that the Supreme Court had "cast doubt on the ability of the elected Congress to protect us against catastrophe" by "improperly set[ting] itself up" as "a super-legislature" that failed to "do justice under the Constitution." His proposed solution was to appoint to the court "younger men who have had personal experiences and contact with modern facts and circumstances" and would outvote the "few men who, being fearful of the future, would deny us the necessary means of dealing with the present." He closed by condemning as insincere those who urged him to seek a constitutional amendment instead. "'Oh!'" FDR claimed they would cry in response to whatever amendment he proposed. "'I was for an amendment all right, but this amendment that you have proposed is not the kind of amendment that I was thinking about.'"[8]

According to a Gallup poll, 30 percent of voters heard the president's March 4 speech and 42 percent heard his March 9 fireside chat. More than one in five voters heard both addresses, and only half heard neither. Sixty-three percent of voters thought his speeches "gained . . . supporters for his plan" rather than "lost supporters" (24 percent). Tellingly, two-thirds agreed that "President Roosevelt should have made his plan an issue in the last election."[9] Letters poured in to the White House. Some, like the vast majority of those sent to members of Congress, were critical. "Yes our government is DIVIDED into 3 branches, but they are not supposed to PULL TOGETHER," wrote a self-described Democrat from Washington State. Others were supportive. "We feel you are working for us," wrote a Californian, "but we did not vote for nor appoint the Supreme Court and we do not feel that they have worked for us." A Pennsylvanian declared, "If I were in your place . . . I would put this Nation under martial law and remove all those old fossils from the bench."[10]

According to political scientist Gregory Caldeira, the two March speeches earned FDR a three-point increase in public support for his court-curbing proposal, but only in the "short run."[11] Each speech rested on a dubious claim, and once the initial enthusiasm faded, this turned out to be more significant. To the Democrats, Roosevelt trumpeted, "We gave warning last November that we had only just begun to fight." In truth, he said nothing about the Supreme Court during his reelection campaign and instead approved a plank in the party platform that mentioned only possible "clarifying amendments." In the fireside chat, FDR claimed, "It is the American people themselves who expect the third horse to pull in unison with the other two"—that is, the Supreme Court pulling with him and Congress—despite considerable evidence that most voters valued an independent judiciary even when they disagreed with some of its decisions. "The number Nine was to be sacred" among voters, complained Secretary of the Interior Harold Ickes, few of whom were old enough to remember when the number of justices was different. "All that is left now is to declare that it is infallible."[12]

"All I had to do was deliver a better speech and the opposition will be beating a path to the White House door," Roosevelt crowed to party chair James Farley in a phone call from Warm Springs, Georgia, where he was vacationing after making his two speeches.[13] Never abandoning his blithe, oft-repeated assumption that "the people are with me," FDR wildly overestimated the lasting effect his speeches would have in both the country and the Senate.[14] The very forthrightness of his argument for expanding the Supreme Court in March only exposed the duplicity of his initial argument in February. Instead of laying the foundation for passage of the court bill, Roosevelt had dug a hole for himself and then, when trying to fill it, raised doubts about the motives behind the whole effort.

While Roosevelt was absent from Washington, an additional problem arose. Both speeches had been timed to coincide with the Senate Judiciary Committee's hearings on the court bill, which began on March 10 with Senator Henry Ashurst, a reluctant supporter, in the chair. The administration's first witness, Attorney General Cummings, trotted out all the original efficiency arguments to justify the plan, even while unwittingly conceding that if a fifteen-member Supreme Court ruled against the administration "because the liberals turned out to be conservatives," then "we would be just where we are now."[15]

Cummings's testimony compounded the problems FDR had created with his original presentation of the bill, after which he wasted a month standing by the deception. Roosevelt undid some of that self-inflicted damage with his two speeches, but the attorney general's testimony undid the undoing. Jackson, the lead witness on the second day of hearings, effectively presented FDR's latest criticism of "judges who resort to a tortured construction of the Constitution."[16] But between them, the two witnesses (Cummings and Jackson) "virtually canceled each other out."[17] In offering a different rationale for the bill, however persuasive, Jackson underscored the president's own mixed messaging. In any event, "it was all too late," Jackson later wrote; "the plan never lived down its initial indirection."[18]

In addition to failing to rouse the voters' support, which he wrongly assumed he could depend on, Roosevelt took for granted organized groups' willingness to mobilize their members and lobby senators to support his bill. In particular, he assumed that the farm, labor, and liberal groups that were part of his first-term coalition would actively engage in the court effort. His decision not to woo them in advance cost him dearly. Farm groups were not of one mind. The Farm Bureau Federation formally supported the bill but was internally divided on the issue. The National Grange opposed it and was united and active.[19] As it turned out, the Supreme Court's overturning of the Agricultural Adjustment Act was not as unpopular as Roosevelt thought.[20] Farmers had profited from Congress's quick passage of the Soil Conservation and Domestic Allotment Act, which restored some of their lost benefits. Liberal groups were focused as much on civil liberties, where the current court's record was generally strong, as on economic issues. They also feared that court packing might turn out to be a Pandora's box whose opening by a future president would lead to the appointment of a dangerously conservative Supreme Court.

Roosevelt was especially disappointed with the labor unions, which had thrived under his administration's policies and enthusiastically supported his reelection campaign. He actually previewed the court bill for John L. Lewis, head of the Congress of Industrial Organizations (CIO), and Charlton Ogburn of the American Federation of Labor (AFL).[21] Lewis expressed his support, but not in the active way the president needed. It was an understandable miscalculation on Roosevelt's part. The CIO had "mounted the most ambitious electoral intervention in American labor history" to reelect Roosevelt in 1936, and he reasonably assumed that labor would remain by his side.[22] But in 1937 unions were preoccupied with their own problems. The AFL, which organized workers by craft as carpenters, plumbers, and so on, was at war with the CIO, which organized them across occupational lines by industry. This fight was of more immediate importance to both groups than FDR's court bill.

A series of sit-down strikes against General Motors, Republic Steel, and other companies—47 strikes in February and 170 by March—eventually involved half a million workers as employees occupied and barricaded factories. These strikes generated a backlash against labor among the public and in Congress. To the extent that unions were active on behalf of the president, concluded Harvard law professor Felix Frankfurter, the "violent aspect of CIO strikes" was an "offsetting source of weakness" for the court bill.[23] Vice President John Nance Garner was so furious with Roosevelt for not denouncing the strikes that, for the first time ever, he left Washington for Texas before the congressional session was over.[24] Conversely, Lewis was upset that the president did not support the strikers.[25] In addition, the Supreme Court's favorable ruling in April on the National Labor Relations Act (discussed later) reduced any urgency unions may have felt about judicial reform. "When they sustained that [law], labor said, 'Well, we have what we want,'" according to Jackson.[26] Making matters worse, with the president's executive reorganization bill sidelined for the duration of the court fight, newspaper publisher Frank Gannett's well-funded Committee to Uphold Constitutional Government was free to devote its media campaign and grassroots organizing efforts "to mobilize and coordinate individual and mass protest against the proposed undermining of an independent judiciary."[27]

Decision 5: Attack the Justices for Acting Politically, but Underestimate Their Political Savvy

For all his certainty that the Supreme Court justices were acting like politicians, it did not occur to Roosevelt that they would break their customary silence on public issues and speak out about his court plan. He was confirmed in this belief when Chief Justice Hughes declined Senator Burton Wheeler's March 18 request to testify about the court bill before the Senate Judiciary Committee. Despite his refusal, Hughes was infuriated by the bill, especially the insinuation that the Supreme Court was behind in its work and needed help from additional, younger justices to catch up. What Roosevelt did not anticipate was that Wheeler and the politically experienced Hughes, with an assist from Justice Louis Brandeis, would find a way for the chief justice to intervene without seeming overtly political. Brandeis was doubly offended by the president's attack on the Supreme Court and by his use of the justices' age as the basis for his concerns about it. "You call up the Chief Justice," Brandeis told Wheeler, an old friend. "He'll give you a letter" that will set the record straight or, as Hughes later put it, convey to the committee "the facts as to the state of the work of the Court." The impatient Brandeis then placed the call himself and put Wheeler on the phone. Hughes invited the senator to visit him at his apartment. On the next day, Sunday, March 21, he handed Wheeler a letter after consulting informally with Brandeis and the conservative Willis Van Devanter about its contents.[28]

"I hope you'll see that this gets wide publicity," Hughes said. "You don't need to worry about that," replied Wheeler.[29] He sprang the letter on the astonished committee the following morning. "The Supreme Court is fully abreast of its work," Hughes's letter began, offering data to demonstrate that "there is no congestion of cases upon our calendar" and citing as evidence Solicitor General Reed's most recent annual report to Congress on the matter. Pretending to take the president at his word about the overriding importance of judicial efficiency, Hughes wrote that, with a larger Supreme Court, "there would be more judges to hear, more judges to confer, more judges to discuss, more judges to be convinced and decide," all of which would "impair that efficiency."[30]

Meanwhile, using statistics privately supplied by Hughes, a *Washington Post* reporter published a series of articles showing that the lower federal courts were no more backlogged because of aging judges than the Supreme Court was.[31] To be sure, the *Post* reported, thirty-four district courts were overworked, but only four of them had judges aged seventy years or older. FDR himself had appointed nine men over age sixty to various circuit courts and was currently seeking confirmation to the Tenth Circuit for Robert L. Williams, who was sixty-eight.[32]

Hughes's letter had a powerful effect. As Corcoran told a colleague, "Hughes has played a bad hand perfectly while we have played a good hand badly."[33] A week later, FDR vented about the chief justice in a letter to Frankfurter, a frequent confidant. "*That* was a characteristic Hughes performance," Roosevelt fumed, "part and parcel of that pretended withdrawal from considerations of policy, while trying to shape them, which is the core of the mischief of which the [court's] majority have so long been guilty."[34] Justice Harlan Fiske Stone was convinced that Hughes had not consulted all his colleagues, some of whom lived close by, before composing the letter because he was eager to get it into Wheeler's hands without running the risk of an extended discussion.[35] Still, there is no question that all nine justices opposed Roosevelt's proposal, and Stone energetically leaked his opposition to journalists and others.[36]

On March 29, one week after the Hughes letter, the Supreme Court handed down a game-changing decision in *West Coast Hotel Co. v. Parrish*, a state minimum wage case that seemed to present the same issues as the previous year's unpopular *Tipaldo* ruling.[37] As in the earlier case, the vote was five to four, but this time Justice Owen Roberts sided with the three liberals and Hughes, who wrote the majority opinion.[38] Several pro–New Deal decisions followed. In especially important rulings, the justices upheld the National Labor Relations Act on April 12 and the Social Security Act on May 24, part of a seventeen-case winning streak (with no losses) for New Deal legislation during the Supreme Court's 1936–1937 term.[39] With his retirement income assured by passage of Sumners's pension bill in March, the oldest of the conservative justices, Van Devanter, announced on May 18 that he intended to step down at the end of the court's current term in June, giving Roosevelt his first opportunity to replace a conservative justice with a liberal one.

That same day, the Senate Judiciary Committee voted ten to eight to recommend rejection of the president's bill; its official report would follow in a month. Caldeira found that, taken together, the National Labor Relations Act decision and Van Devanter's retirement "spelled doom for FDR's bill" in the court of public opinion, where support declined almost 10 percent in response to these events.[40]

On June 2, 1936, one day after the *Tipaldo* ruling, Roosevelt said the Supreme Court had placed the country in "no man's land." Now, at a press briefing the day after the National Labor Relations Act decision, he declared that "no man's land has been eliminated but see what we have in place of it: we are now in 'Roberts's land.'"[41] FDR told Farley he was "convinced now more than ever that the proposals for reform of the Court are warranted."[42] Having moved from right to left, the president argued, Roberts might turn rightward again—who knew? As far as FDR was concerned, the need for additional justices was confirmed, not eliminated, by the Supreme Court's unpredictable behavior, which, according to a frustrated Jackson, "impressed the president, rather unfortunately, as weakness rather than strength."[43] "And now, with the switch by Roberts," Frankfurter wrote to FDR, "even a blind man ought to see that the Court is in politics."[44] Others regarded *Parrish* as another nail in the court bill's coffin. Public support for the measure had never been high, and that situation did not improve. Roberts's "switch in time," some quipped, had "saved nine."[45]

Forests have been laid bare to print the books and articles debating Roberts's change of course. Myriad law professors—so-called internalists—have seen the justice's vote in *West Coast Hotel Co. v. Parrish* as an extension of his previous jurisprudence, citing, for example, his liberal ruling in the 1934 case *Nebbia v. New York*.[46] Historians and political scientists (externalists) have typically seen the change as Roberts's concession to political reality.[47] One aspect of this dispute, at least, has been settled. Roberts's vote in *Parrish*, although not announced until late March 1937, was cast the previous December 19, when the court, having just heard oral arguments, decided to hold off announcing its decision until Justice Stone returned to the bench after a serious illness. Clearly, it was not the introduction of Roosevelt's court bill six weeks later that triggered Roberts's change of mind. Nor was the November 1936 election the likely cause. Roberts apparently voted to grant certiorari in the case in October—something he would not have done unless he intended to change sides.[48] FDR later invoked *post hoc ergo propter hoc* reasoning to argue that "it would be a little naïve to refuse to recognize some connection between these 1937 decisions and the Supreme Court fight."[49] In truth, Roberts's initial switch came before the court fight began and therefore could not have been caused by it.

All that being said, Roberts's switch was likely politically motivated. As long as he still thought he had a chance to win the Republican presidential nomination at the party's June 9–12, 1936, convention, Roberts had every incentive to side with the court's four conservatives. He assumed—wrongly, as it turned out—that conservative Republican politicians would continue to support the conservative justices' decisions to overturn New Deal–style legislation even when enacted by state governments—in this case, New York's law requiring a minimum wage for women workers. The *Tipaldo* case was decided on May 2 and announced on June 1, both dates falling in the preconvention period when Roberts's hopes for the nomination were still alive. Like Hughes, who was an associate justice when he left the court to become the GOP nominee for president in 1916, Roberts served in an era when the Supreme Court was one of several plausible stepping-stones to the presidency. Years later, he mused about the temptations faced by politically ambitious justices and the encouragement he received to run for president, even though "I turned a hard face on that thing."[50] He even urged passage of a constitutional amendment stating that "no Chief Justice or associate justice of the Supreme Court shall be eligible to the office of President or Vice President," either while serving on the court or afterward.[51] One cannot help but think that, as Queen Gertrude says of another character in *Hamlet*, Roberts "doth protest too much."

In any case, when Roberts failed to get the Republican Party's presidential nomination, his political incentive to side with the court's conservatives was extinguished. Clearly his future was with the court, not the GOP. He was free to do what Hughes wanted him to do—that is, take the Supreme Court out of the political line of fire by ending its campaign against the New Deal. Hughes rejoiced when Roberts told him how he planned to vote in *Parrish*, barely resisting the temptation to hug him.[52]

Regardless of how one explains Roberts's decision to vote with the liberals on major New Deal cases in 1937, the new judicial reality brought about by his switch created a new political reality for Roosevelt's court bill. With the Senate increasingly unlikely to see the urgency of authorizing the appointment of six new justices, what would the president decide to do next?

Decision 6: Do Not Compromise—Until It Is Too Late

"Why run for a train after you've caught it?" Senator James Byrnes of South Carolina, a staunch Roosevelt supporter, asked after the Supreme Court began to rule in the administration's favor. On April 13 Senate majority leader Joseph Robinson sent word to the White House that "the [court] bill's raising hell in the Senate . . . but if the president wants to compromise I can get him a couple of extra justices tomorrow."[53] Roosevelt's "Roberts's land" comment that same day demonstrated his lack of interest in changing course. He offered the same refusal one month later when Robinson and the two House Democratic leaders, Speaker William Bankhead and majority leader Sam Rayburn, told him on May 14 that his best bet would be to put the court bill aside so Congress could take up other New Deal legislation. (The president was getting the same message from aides Jackson, Cohen, and Corcoran.)[54] Robinson also warned that the Senate Judiciary Committee, despite its fifteen-to-three Democratic majority, was about to issue a severely adverse report on the court bill to buttress its recommendation that the Senate reject it.[55]

Once again, Roosevelt dismissed their concerns. "The people are with me," he repeated, newly emboldened by a recent trip to Texas. While there, he met with Lyndon B. Johnson, who had just won the Democratic primary for a House seat based on a relentless campaign in favor of court packing. The fact that Johnson had received only 28 percent of the vote against half a dozen other candidates did not faze either him or the president. FDR was grasping at straws. As Rayburn, who knew Texas better than anyone, told him, the state legislature's near-unanimous decision to condemn the court plan was a more reliable indicator of public opinion than Johnson's 8,280 votes in the primary. Meanwhile, Roosevelt continued to tell senators and others that he wanted to appoint justices who, unlike even the three liberals currently on the Supreme Court, would be "friendly and approachable," open to informal consultation about his "great plans for social and economic reform."[56]

Roosevelt's refusal to accept a two-justice compromise was motivated in large part by his unwillingness to acknowledge the obvious decline in public and congressional support for his own plan, the more cooperative behavior of the Supreme Court, and the opportunity afforded by Van Devanter's retirement. That said, his position was not altogether unreasonable.[57] Van Devanter's seat had been promised to the sixty-five-year-old Robinson, whom colleagues of both parties gathered on the Senate floor to congratulate as "Mr. Justice" the moment the vacancy was announced. Robinson had been an unflaggingly loyal Senate majority leader, but Roosevelt feared that his underlying conservatism might emerge once he was on the court. If Hughes and Roberts reverted to their previous anti–New Deal jurisprudence and Robinson joined them and the three remaining conservatives, even two new liberal appointees could not outvote a six-to-five conservative majority.[58] Roosevelt calculated that he needed at least four new justices, assuming he was willing to compromise at all.

By the time Roosevelt finally realized he had no choice but to compromise, it may have been too late. On June 14 the Judiciary Committee issued its brutally negative report on the court bill, branding it "needless, futile, and utterly dangerous" and recommending that it "should be so emphatically rejected that its parallel will never again be presented to the free representatives of the free people of America."[59] The bill's eight Democratic supporters on the committee, outvoted by seven fellow Democrats and three Republicans, offered no defense. As Jeff Shesol observes, the report painted Roosevelt "as a liar, as power mad, as hellbent on crushing the Court and wrecking the Constitution."[60] No report from a congressional committee controlled by the president's party has ever condemned a presidential proposal so harshly.

Anticipating a bad (but not that bad) committee report, Roosevelt summoned Robinson to the White House. FDR had already told Secretary of the Treasury Henry Morgenthau that if he had three vacancies, he "might be able to sandwich in Joe Robinson."[61] The president now indicated to Robinson that his own appointment to the Supreme Court hinged on his ability to work out an acceptable compromise in the Senate, and not just for two or three new justices. "If there was to be a bride there must also be bridesmaids—at least four of them," he said.[62] As political scientist James MacGregor Burns argues, it was a brutally effective maneuver: "if the senators wanted to help their old colleague, they would have to provide some extra appointments as well."[63] Energized, Robinson embraced a substitute measure offered by Senator Carl Hatch of New Mexico that would add a new member to the Supreme Court for every justice who was aged seventy-five or older. If adopted, this would expand the membership not to fifteen but to twelve, and at a pace of one new appointment per year, rather than all at once.

Having passed up earlier opportunities for compromise, Roosevelt now decided he could settle for the Hatch substitute. Barring a filibuster, which opponents could wage successfully by holding the floor for hours at a time and introducing dozens of amendments to Hatch's bill, Robinson thought he could swing enough votes to prevail.[64] If so, they would be based on loyalty to, affection for, and favors owed to Robinson, not the president. Overweight and in poor health, suffering in the brutal heat of an unusually severe Washington summer, and hectored by interruptions from court-packing opponents, Robinson waged his battle for passage on the Senate floor until July 13. That night, he left the Capitol exhausted, returned to his solitary, unair-conditioned apartment, and died of a heart attack. Although Roosevelt resolved to fight on, he did not join the thirty-eight senators who rode a train to Arkansas to attend Robinson's July 18 funeral. That round trip devolved into an anti-Roosevelt, anti-court-packing caucus, fueled by resentment over the president's decision not to announce Robinson's appointment to the Supreme Court unless he rammed the compromise bill through the Senate and stoked by his decision not to attend the funeral. It undid much of the goodwill Roosevelt had earned by inviting all 407 Democratic members of Congress to a June 25 weekend "frolic" at the Jefferson Island Club off the Maryland coast.

When FDR met with Vice President Garner, who returned to Washington on the funeral train on July 20, to learn how things stood in the Senate, Garner asked the president, "Do you want it with the bark on or the bark off?" "The rough way," Roosevelt replied. "You're licked,

Cap'n," said Garner. "You haven't gotten the votes."[65] Roosevelt accepted Garner's verdict, along with his offer to try to persuade Congress to salvage other parts of the bill. As Garner explained the terms of surrender to Senator Wheeler, "The Supreme Court [is] out of it, no roving judges, no Supreme Court proctor."[66]

Two days later, on July 22, the Senate voted seventy to twenty to recommit the president's bill to the Judiciary Committee, with instructions to focus on "judicial reform" of the lower federal courts, not the Supreme Court. In an effort to save face for the president, Democratic senator and Judiciary Committee member Marvel Logan of Kentucky did not explicitly refer to the Supreme Court when making the recommittal motion. This prompted progressive Republican Hiram Johnson of California to ask, "The Supreme Court is out of the way?" "The Supreme Court is out of the way," Logan acknowledged. "Glory be to God!" exclaimed Johnson, prompting widespread applause in the chamber.[67]

Fifty-three of the seventy-one Democrats whose votes were recorded supported recommittal, along with every Republican. Publicly, Roosevelt accepted defeat with good grace, even claiming credit for the Supreme Court's liberal turn. To fill the Van Devanter vacancy, he appointed an ardent New Dealer: Senator Hugo Black of Alabama. Privately, FDR resolved to seek political vengeance against Democratic opponents of the court bill who were on the ballot in the 1938 midterm elections. He rued his March 4 declaration that he had no ambition to seek a third term, certain that its main effect had been to encourage conservatives in the party to regard him as a lame duck. Three years later, Roosevelt would rescind his preemptive withdrawal from the 1940 election, but in the meantime, he opened the door for Vice President Garner to step forward as both a "lightning rod for conservative protests during the second term" and a contender for the presidential nomination on behalf of conservative Democrats.[68]

Decision 7: Sacrifice the Executive Reorganization Bill to Campaign for the Court Bill

No one could have predicted that the first year of the Seventy-Fifth Congress, led by a reelected president with three-fourths majorities in both chambers, would be so unproductive. Yet long before he died, Senator Robinson described it as the least productive session he could remember. FDR's failed campaign for his court bill supplanted everything else. When Robinson and his fellow Democratic leaders in the House visited Roosevelt on May 14 to urge him to postpone the court bill so that other items on the president's agenda could be considered, FDR turned them down flat.

Roosevelt's executive reorganization bill was one casualty of his undiluted focus on the Supreme Court. Like the court bill, it was "literally sprung on Congress" without advance consultation.[69] Still, when it was introduced in January, Congress seemed receptive to the creation of a new Executive Office of the President. To secure passage of those parts of the bill empowering the president to overhaul the existing executive departments and agencies, however, Roosevelt had work to do. But because this measure concerned the executive branch of government, which, unlike the Supreme Court, did not enjoy public esteem for its constitutional independence, it was exactly the sort of work he could accomplish by making a sustained effort.

Instead, the reorganization bill was dead in 1937, collateral damage from the court fight. It would not return to the president's agenda until 1939, and even then in diluted form. In the meantime, Roosevelt nursed his anger. "For weeks and months I found him fuming against the members of his own party he blamed for his bucket of bitterness," observed Farley.[70] FDR set his sights on 1938.

CHAPTER 6

Did FDR Succeed?

Franklin D. Roosevelt's presidential ambitions extended well beyond his own election in 1932 and reelection in 1936 (and, as it turned out, in 1940 and 1944 as well). Those ambitions also exceeded the dramatic alterations in public policy—broadly speaking, the expanded federal role in the economy known as the New Deal—that he was able to enact. FDR wanted nothing less than to embed these transformations enduringly in the major institutions of national government and politics. Under the Constitution, with its system of "separated institutions sharing powers," controlling one or even two branches was not enough.[1] His complaint that the "three-horse team" of Congress, the executive, and the Supreme Court was not pulling together was grounded in a strong conviction that constitutional government functions well only when all three move in the same direction at the same time and at the same pace. FDR was president, but unless he could yoke together legislators, judges, and the rest of the executive branch in lasting ways, he argued, "the field will not be ploughed."[2] The yoke in this metaphor was the Democratic Party, the extragovernmental institution that, in alliance with the president, could serve as the binding element and driving force of the three constitutional power centers.

To what extent did Roosevelt succeed in achieving this goal? The verdict is mixed. In every case—the Supreme Court, the executive branch bureaucracy, Congress, and the Democratic Party—he was a highly consequential president whose influence endured long beyond his tenure. But in no case did FDR achieve the mastery he sought. The imperfectly yoked horses of government sometimes functioned as a team, but their individual wills were never broken.

The Supreme Court

Despite the testimony of close aides who said the president felt "thoroughly beaten" in the court fight, "was completely humiliated" by his defeat, and was "very obsessive" about it, FDR later claimed that when it came to the Supreme Court, "we lost the battle but we won the war."[3] "The Court yielded," he gloated. "The Court changed. . . . What a change!"[4] Clearly, the justices' decision in *West Coast Hotel Co. v. Parrish* marked the start of a liberal turn in jurisprudence.[5] Never again would the Supreme Court overturn a federal law that constrained business. In fact, "in ten terms from 1937 through 1946," observed historian William Leuchtenburg, "the Court reversed thirty-two of its earlier decisions."[6]

Would this transformation in the Supreme Court's approach to the New Deal have taken place if Roosevelt had not tried to increase the number of justices from nine to fifteen? As shown in chapter 5, Justice Owen Roberts's crucial votes in *Parrish*—first to grant certiorari in October 1936 and then, two months later, to side with the liberals in the case's disposition—were registered well before Roosevelt introduced his court bill in February 1937. In fact, the vote granting certiorari came before the November 1936 election and was cast at a time when the outcome of that contest, much less the magnitude of Roosevelt's victory, appeared doubtful. Roosevelt ducked the issue of the Supreme Court during the entire campaign, leaving voters with the understandable impression that he had no intention of doing anything about it.

What apparently influenced Roberts was his realization in June 1936 that he was not going to be the Republican nominee for president and therefore would not benefit politically by continuing to oppose the New Deal. He had already laid the foundation for a more liberal jurisprudence in the 1934 case *Nebbia v. New York*, in which he offered an expansive reading of government's constitutional power to legislate in "the common interest."[7] Returning to this approach in 1937 was not as dramatic a "switch" for Roberts as it would have been for any of the four avowedly conservative justices.[8]

Beginning in May 1937 with Justice Willis Van Devanter's announced retirement, a series of vacancies occurred on the nine-member Supreme Court that Roosevelt was able to fill in the customary way. After a four-year lag in turnover, vacancies were bound to arise, especially considering that six of the justices were at least seventy years old. Representative Hatton Sumners's bill to guarantee the income of retired justices, which became law in March 1937, made the prospect of stepping down more attractive to members whose service on the relatively low-paying court had come at some financial sacrifice.[9] The administration's legal team, sometimes ineffective in its written and oral arguments during the New Deal's early years, had grown in skill, knowledge, and competence in the latter part of Roosevelt's first term. New Deal laws were more carefully crafted to survive judicial scrutiny. Chief Justice Charles Evans Hughes even hinted that these improvements alone would have led to more proadministration decisions if FDR had been patient.[10] Beyond that, as Senator Henry Ashurst told the president, urging a different kind of patience, "Father Time" was on his side.[11]

Opportunities soon arose. During FDR's first fifty months as president, no justices died or retired; thereafter, vacancies occurred on the court at a rate of one every eight months for the remainder of his time as president. By 1941, the first year of his third term, seven of the nine justices were Roosevelt appointees (all but Roberts and Hughes), the most chosen by a president since George Washington. Van Devanter's exit was followed by that of George Sutherland (who retired) and Benjamin Cardozo (who died) in 1938; Louis Brandeis (retired) and Pierce Butler (died) in 1939; James McReynolds and Charles Evans Hughes (both retired) in 1941, enabling Roosevelt to promote Harlan Fiske Stone to chief justice and appoint Stone's and McReynolds's successors as associate justices; and James Byrnes, a 1941 Roosevelt appointee who, bored with the job, left the court in 1942 to head the wartime Office of Economic Stabilization.

As these justices vacated their seats, Roosevelt nominated their replacements, all of whom were confirmed by the Senate. Senator Hugo Black of Alabama replaced Van Devanter, Solicitor General Stanley Reed replaced Sutherland, law professor Felix Frankfurter replaced Cardozo,

Securities and Exchange Commission chair William O. Douglas replaced Brandeis, Governor Frank Murphy of Michigan replaced Butler, Senator Byrnes of South Carolina replaced McReynolds, Attorney General Robert H. Jackson replaced Stone when Stone replaced Hughes as chief, and appeals court judge Wiley Rutledge replaced Byrnes. Roosevelt, who publicly commented on Supreme Court cases more frequently and negatively than all of his predecessors combined in 1936 and, especially, 1937, made many fewer and much more positive comments for the rest of his time in office.[12]

FDR's appointees to the Supreme Court (none during his first term, nine during his second and third) shared three common characteristics. One was their liberalism, which had been well established before he chose them. Another was their relative youth; their average age at the time of their appointment was fifty, which increased the likelihood that Roosevelt's imprint on the court would endure well into the future.[13] The third characteristic was that most of their previous experience was in politics and government: senator, governor, cabinet or subcabinet member.[14] Only Rutledge had relevant judicial experience—two years as a federal appeals court judge—before joining the Supreme Court.

FDR's appointments of justices whose background was political rather than judicial did not provoke charges that he was politicizing the court. As discussed in chapter 3, drawing justices from the ranks of politically prominent leaders was nothing new; the practice had prevailed for nearly all of American history. Ironically, it was in subsequent generations, when presidents began to limit the pool of potential appointees largely to federal appellate judges, that efforts to undo the court's allegedly political character reemerged. The Supreme Court that progressives wanted to pack in the early 2020s consisted of eight federal appeals court judges and a law school dean. Six of them had clerked for a justice early in their legal career. None had ever held or even sought an elected office.

Other parts of Roosevelt's judicial reform bill (admittedly, the parts he did not care much about) survived the death of its court-packing provisions. On July 29, 1937, a week after the Senate voted to recommit the bill, the Judiciary Committee endorsed the revised Judicial Procedures

Reform Act passed by the House, led by Representative Sumners. This new legislation addressed aspects of the previous bill's goal of revising the lower courts, but without adding any new federal judges. Specifically, the act denied district court judges the right to enjoin a federal statute on constitutional grounds, except when meeting as a three-member panel; authorized the attorney general to be notified of and enter into lawsuits between private parties that involved constitutional issues; and empowered the chief judge in each circuit (not a Supreme Court–appointed proctor) to reassign district court judges based on need.[15] "It presents meritorious provisions of a minor character," Attorney General Homer Cummings advised the president, who signed the bill on August 26.[16] But FDR did so sourly, "with bad grace," according to adviser Rexford Tugwell.[17]

These modest changes in the federal judiciary ended Roosevelt's effort to reform the federal courts legislatively, along with broader efforts to amend the Constitution. Ashurst's "Father Time," Sumners's retirement act, and Roberts's abandoned presidential ambition, not Roosevelt's court-packing campaign, turned the Supreme Court around. FDR's reelection in 1936 and 1940 made it clear to the conservative justices that in matters that did not threaten the court's status as an independent branch, the voters sided with the president, not with them. FDR was gratified by the Supreme Court's embrace of the "Constitutional Revolution of 1937."[18] Within the span of a decade, conservative rulings by the court fell from more than 80 percent of its cases to less than 20 percent—that is, from an all-time high in the twentieth century to an all-time low in that century (and ever since).[19] But Roosevelt could not have been pleased by the failed court-curbing campaign's effect on his larger effort to embed the New Deal enduringly not just in the judiciary but also in the executive branch, Congress, and the Democratic Party.

The Executive Branch

Three months after losing the Supreme Court fight in July 1937, Roosevelt summoned Congress into special session on November 15 and urged it to enact several items from his legislative agenda, including the executive reorganization bill. By the time the session ended on December 21, nothing had been accomplished. Still bitter, the president nonetheless accepted that, in contrast to his inflexibility regarding the Supreme Court, bending would be better than breaking when it came reorganization. Responding to pressure from powerful organized groups and their allies on Capitol Hill, in early 1938 he agreed to exempt favored agencies, such as the Veterans Bureau and the Office of Education, from being absorbed into any of the cabinet departments. He also conceded that Congress could overturn any reorganization plan he proposed by a simple majority rather than a two-thirds vote of both houses if it acted within sixty days of receiving the plan.

Roosevelt's concessions had little effect. Memories of his court-packing campaign were still fresh, and in the minds of the public and members of Congress, executive reorganization was linked with fears that the president was seeking dictatorial power. Roosevelt felt compelled to state: "A. I have no inclination to be a dictator. B. I have none of the qualifications which would make me a successful dictator."[20] He was right. As president-elect in 1933, he had resisted influential calls for him to assume dictatorial powers during the brief moment when European strongmen were much admired for their ability to get things done. Yet now, five years later, with the horrors of Mussolini's invasion of Ethiopia, Hitler's remilitarization of the Rhineland, and Stalin's purge-style show trials much in the news, Roosevelt faced charges that he intended to emulate them. In particular, Democratic senator Burton Wheeler of Montana, Republican senator Hiram Johnson of California, and other strongly isolationist progressives in both parties who had supported FDR's first-term domestic policies worried that, in light of these developments in Europe, he would try to involve the United States in global affairs during his second term. They resisted any increases in presidential power that might enhance his ability to do so.[21]

The Senate grudgingly passed a much-diminished version of the reorganization bill on March 28, 1938, by a vote of forty-nine to forty-two. On April 8 the House voted to send the president's version of the bill back to committee, the same fate dealt to his court plan less than a year before in the Senate. More than one hundred House Democrats voted for recommittal. As they had with the court plan, Republicans voted against the bill but allowed Democrats to take the lead in public opposition.[22]

Roosevelt revived executive reorganization in 1939, diluting his plan sufficiently to satisfy every specific objection. More agencies were exempted from the bill's coverage—a total of twenty-one, including all the independent regulatory commissions. The cozy relationships between individual agencies, the congressional committees and subcommittees that oversaw them, and the interest groups most affected by their actions—variously dubbed "iron triangles," "subgovernments," or "subsystems" by political scientists—were largely unaffected. Roosevelt's hopes for a new Department of Welfare and Department of Public Works and for an expanded Interior Department rebranded as the Department of Conservation were abandoned. His reorganization authority, still subject to congressional veto, was limited to two years. The Civil Service Commission remained independent, and his original plan to expand civil service coverage within the federal workforce was shelved. Responsibility for auditing government expenditures remained with the congressionally appointed comptroller general and Government Accounting Office rather than becoming an executive responsibility. In general, Roosevelt replaced his original rationale for reorganization—enhanced managerial control of the bureaucracy by the president—with an emphasis on greater economy and efficiency, using language embraced by Senator Harry F. Byrd of Virginia and other congressional conservatives. The House approved the watered-down reorganization bill by a vote of 246 to 153 on March 8, 1939, and the Senate passed it 63 to 23 on March 22.

The Reorganization Act of 1939 accomplished far less than Roosevelt would have been able to persuade Congress to accept in 1937 if he had not paired reorganization with the court bill and devoted all his efforts to the latter. Even so, the 1939 act planted acorns of transformation in the presidency that grew into mighty oaks after Roosevelt left office. One item that remained intact in the final bill was the authorization to hire six presidential assistants, which, as political scientist John P. Burke points out, "was the opening wedge in the creation of a large-scale presidential staff" consisting mostly of specialized experts, not the wide-ranging generalists on whom Roosevelt tended to rely.[23] The White House staff nearly quadrupled in size from 61 to 223 under Roosevelt's successor,

Harry S. Truman, and it all but doubled again, to 411, by the time John F. Kennedy took office in 1961.[24] The other lasting feature of Roosevelt's reorganization initiative was the creation of the Executive Office of the President, with the Bureau of the Budget (BOB) at its center.[25] Like the expanded White House staff, BOB's value to presidents became apparent starting with Truman, who made it "the prime source of presidential staff work on the administration's legislative program." The bureau was charged with coordinating all executive branch recommendations and imposing "central clearance" on every newly proposed bill before it was sent to Congress and every newly passed bill before the president signed it.[26] As political scientist Herbert Emmerich aptly wrote, the process by which the modest 1939 act was transformed into major institutional change after FDR left office turned "ashes into phoenix."[27]

Congress

By the time Roosevelt's efforts to impose his will on the Supreme Court and the executive branch had run their course, nothing and everything had changed on Capitol Hill. Both the House of Representatives and the Senate remained three-fourths Democratic through the end of 1938, but FDR's relationship with both chambers dramatically worsened. Not a single domestic policy on the scale of Roosevelt's first-term relief and reform measures was enacted by the Seventy-Fifth Congress or its successors.[28] Major legislation that seemed certain to pass at the start of the 1937 session—notably, the reorganization bill, a farm bill to replace the Agricultural Adjustment Act, and an extension of the Tennessee Valley Authority model to seven other regions—fell by the wayside. Only the Fair Labor Standards Act of 1938, a watered-down bill to impose a minimum wage and maximum hours on some but not all sectors of the economy, became law. It was the last New Deal domestic policy ever enacted.[29]

Of all the major institutions of government Roosevelt sought to master in lasting ways, Congress was the one he thought was already securely in his domain, thanks to his long coattails in the 1932, 1934, and 1936 elections. But in the aftermath of his second-term court-packing and executive reorganization campaigns, multiple progressive Democrats, Republicans, and independent legislators who had supported FDR's previous New Deal programs ceased to do so.[30] Congressional conservatives in both parties, including southern Democrats who had voted (in some cases reluctantly) for items in his first-term agenda, now formed a long-term alliance in opposition to the president: the so-called Conservative Coalition.[31]

Roosevelt's new opponents in Congress were variously motivated. Western progressives, wary of any centralized concentration of power, recoiled at what they perceived as the president's grab at control of the entire government. Southern conservatives who had been pleased to support FDR's early spending programs because they poured federal money into their impoverished states and districts were increasingly worried that his agenda now included disrupting their region's regime of white racial hegemony. Republicans welcomed any alliance that would rein in the Democratic president and arrest their party's political decline.

Roosevelt was not defeated by Congress; indeed, the growing foreign policy crises that dominated the remainder of his time in office, culminating in World War II, had the traditional effect of enhancing presidential ascendancy. Beyond that, the growth in the number and complexity of domestic programs that marked FDR's first term necessarily involved delegations of discretionary authority from Congress to the "administrative presidency" to implement these new programs.[32] But the fallout from the failed court-packing and executive reorganization campaigns meant that Roosevelt's effort to attain enduring liberal mastery over Congress was only partly successful. The bipartisan alliance between conservative Republicans and southern Democrats in Congress lasted into the 1960s, thwarting the domestic reform efforts of every Democratic president who followed for more than a generation, including Truman's Fair Deal and Kennedy's New Fronter. In the 1980s a substantial southern cadre of so-called Boll Weevil Democrats became an essential component of Republican president Ronald Reagan's first-term legislative majority, and in the 1990s a similar group, now known as the Blue Dog Democrats, obstructed the liberal elements of Democratic president Bill Clinton's reform agenda, even when their party enjoyed majorities in both congressional chambers.

The Democratic Party

During his first term, FDR elevated the Democratic Party to majority status for the first time since Andrew Jackson did so a century before. He also launched the effort to remake it as the nation's liberal party, triumphing over conservative opponents such as Al Smith and John W. Davis, the party's two most recent presidential nominees, and thereby giving Democrats an ideological identity that had previously been diffuse. This effort made conservative southern whites nervous. They were not happy when FDR persuaded the party's 1936 national convention to abandon the two-thirds rule for presidential nominations, denying the South the ability to veto candidates it found unacceptable. And they especially did not like taking a backseat to the party's northern coalition of unionized workers, urban Catholics and Jews, liberals, and Blacks.

FDR took his defeats on executive reorganization and, especially, court packing hard. He placed most of the blame on the Democrats in Congress whose opposition had doomed those measures. Progressive Democratic opponents of the bills at least supported his broader effort to liberalize the party, but the conservatives who opposed the bills also opposed his overall vision for it. Roosevelt's first chance to show them who was boss came in the next round of elections, the midterm Democratic primary contests in 1938. All members of the House of Representatives and about one-third of senators were on the ballot. According to speechwriter Samuel Rosenman, FDR felt "a very, very strong animus against certain of the congressional members who led the fight against him or joined the fight against him," and he targeted several Democratic opponents of his bills by supporting their pro–New Deal challengers.[33] He was, said Rosenman, so driven by "personal resentment at the two major legislative defeats dealt him by members of his own party" that he was "blinded . . . to the great dangers to his own standing and prestige that were inherent in his entry into purely local primary party contests."[34] FDR's resentment was "not cooled by the lapse of time, but glowed as fierce as ever," wrote Democratic National Committee chair James Farley.[35]

The extent to which Roosevelt's intervention in Democratic primaries was regarded as a shocking departure from the norm was indicated by the label the press gave it: "the purge." The term evoked Stalin's elimination of suspected opponents in the Soviet Communist Party and military. Roosevelt announced his intention in a fireside chat on June 24, 1938. "As the head of the Democratic Party," he said, "I feel that I have every right to speak in those few instances where there may be a clear issue between candidates for a Democratic nomination." His list of targeted candidates—"Copperheads," he called them, the label applied to northern Democrats who sympathized with the South during the Civil War—included a few northerners, notably House Rules Committee chair John O'Connor of New York and senators Guy Gillette of Iowa and Frederick Van Nuys of Indiana. But his main targets were in the South: Walter F. George of Georgia, Ellison "Cotton Ed" Smith of South Carolina, and Millard Tydings of Maryland in the Senate and Howard Smith of Virginia and Eugene Cox of Georgia in the House. FDR actively campaigned in the primaries, urging Democratic voters to reject incumbent Democratic officeholders in favor of his preferred candidates. He already had stirred up white southerners by describing their society as "feudal" and adding, "When you come right down to it, there is little difference between the feudal system and the fascist system. If you believe in one, you lean to the other."[36]

All of Roosevelt's targeted opponents but O'Connor won their primaries, usually by substantial majorities. Until then, it was unclear whether conservative Democrats could fend off opposition from the president. Now, with proof that they could, others in the party were emboldened to think they could chart their own course without worrying about incurring Roosevelt's wrath. Even worse, the intraparty divisions fomented by FDR, along with an economic recession that cost four million workers their jobs, contributed to the Democrats' massive losses to the Republicans in the November midterm election: eighty seats in the House, eight seats in the Senate, and thirteen governorships.

The losses fell most heavily among liberal northern Democrats. The South remained monochromatically Democratic and increasingly conservative. The seventeen-point majority enjoyed by self-identified Democratic voters over Republicans in 1937 shrank to four points two years later.[37] To be sure, the Democrats remained the nation's majority party even after experiencing their worst midterm losses of the century—a record of defeat that has yet to be surpassed. Despite these losses, both houses of Congress remained in Democratic hands. The long-run effects of Roosevelt's presidency on the party were, on balance, both positive and liberalizing. The former effect would continue through the 1960s. The latter is more evident than ever in the present.

Conclusion

FDR's historical reputation is secure. At last count, presidential scholars have been asked to rate the presidents twenty-three times since the first such survey was conducted in 1948. In every one of them, FDR ranked first, second, or third, rivaled only by George Washington and Abraham Lincoln.[38] Most scholars would agree, however, that these assessments are based on his first and third terms, in which "Dr. New Deal" addressed the Depression and "Dr. Win-the-War" led the United States to victory in World War II.[39] FDR's second term, despite being ushered in by a forty-six-state landslide victory and a three-fourths Democratic majority in Congress, was singularly marked by disappointment: the failed court and reorganization bills in 1937, the resulting emergence of the Conservative Coalition in Congress, the botched purge of fellow Democrats, the dramatic losses in the 1938 midterm elections, and the failure of Congress to enact significant domestic legislation.

More than anything else, Roosevelt's second-term disappointments were the product of his "vaulting ambition," which caused him to "o'erleap" the mandate of the 1936 election.[40] In seeking a second term, FDR asked the voters to conduct a referendum on his first-term performance—that is, to make their decision retrospectively, not prospectively. He left the Supreme Court issue out of the campaign entirely and so muted his party platform's stance on the judiciary that it ended up being less reformist than the Republican platform. He underestimated—as would conservative critics of the Warren Court in the 1960s and liberal critics of the Roberts Court in the 2020s—the public's deeply rooted resistance to structural alterations of the Supreme Court.[41] In the short term, Roosevelt ignored polls demonstrating the public's high regard for the Hughes Court even when they disagreed with some of its decisions. "The court reform bill was like throwing a stone through a cathedral window," said Robert Jackson.[42]

Yet FDR acted as if he had done none of these things. As late as 1941, he claimed, "The spirit of the Democratic campaign [in 1936] was expressed in my speech at Madison Square Garden in New York City on October 31, 1936: that for all our objectives—many of which had been blocked by the Supreme Court—we had 'only just begun to fight.'"[43] In truth, this was the only campaign speech of its kind that he delivered. The others took the economic improvements that occurred between "four years ago and now" as their theme. In all, after the election, "there was too much feeling within the administration that it really didn't need to consult with anybody," said Jackson. "The feeling of almost infallibility, the overconfidence that succeeded the 1936 election, was probably the dominant cause of the mishandling of the [court] proposal."[44]

Roosevelt's o'erleaping was hardly unique. It seems more than coincidental that the four presidents who won the largest reelection victories in modern history, thereby demonstrating their sensitivity to public opinion, instantly breached the bounds of permissible presidential conduct in ways that incurred the public's wrath. Roosevelt's court-packing proposal in 1937, Lyndon B. Johnson's escalation of the Vietnam War in 1965, the continuing cover-up of the Watergate scandal by Richard Nixon in 1973, and Ronald Reagan's Iran-contra scandal in 1985 all involved presidential overreach—as did Donald Trump's effort to overturn the 2020 election, which in his mind (if nowhere else) he won by a "landslide." Compounding their problems, each of these presidents then circled the wagons, all of them driven by deferential aides, to seal out unpleasant but necessary political information and advice when their initiatives went sour. From the heights of political unity and consensus following their landslide reelections, FDR, LBJ, Nixon, and Reagan descended into varying depths of stalemate during their second terms.

The common feature of each of these presidents' self-inflicted political wounds was their erroneous conclusion that the voters had granted them blanket authorization to rule as they saw fit. In truth, the voters had merely endorsed these presidents' conduct during their first terms, expressed a lack of confidence in their opponents, and shown faith that they would continue to skillfully lead one branch in a three-branch government. Handily reelected second-term presidents have been equally prone to take congressional support for granted at the very time that members of Congress have grown weary of four years of pressure from the president and White House staff. In the face of even mild resistance in Congress, second-term presidents tend to rely on executive orders and other unilateral actions instead of legislative persuasion and compromise. There is nothing inevitable about such a reaction from future presidents, but the temptations of vaulting ambition are not easy to resist.

NOTES

PREFACE

1. Laurence Tribe and Nancy Gertner, "The Supreme Court Isn't Well: The Only Hope for a Cure Is More Justices," *Washington Post*, December 9, 2021.

2. Inae Oh, "Progressives Turn up the Heat on Biden to Do Literally Anything about the Supreme Court," *Mother Jones*, June 26, 2022, https://www.moth erjones.com/politics/2022/06/biden-filibuster-expand-court-roe/.

PROLOGUE: JANUARY 6, 1937

1. The practice of having one cabinet member in the presidential line of succession—a "designated survivor"—not attend the State of the Union address did not begin until 1981.

2. Franklin D. Roosevelt, "Annual Message to Congress, January 6, 1937," American Presidency Project, https://www.presidency.ucsb.edu/documents/an nual-message-congress-1.

3. Franklin D. Roosevelt, "Fireside Chat, March 9, 1937," American Presidency Project, https://www.presidency.ucsb.edu/documents/fireside-chat-17.

4. William Shakespeare, *Macbeth*, act I, scene 7, ll. 25–28.

CHAPTER 1. FDR, THE EXECUTIVE BRANCH, AND THE SUPREME COURT: RELIEF, REFORM, AND RESISTANCE

1. Peverill Squire, "Why the 1936 *Literary Digest* Poll Failed," *Public Opinion Quarterly* 52 (Spring 1968): 125–133.

2. Doris Kearns Goodwin, *Leadership in Turbulent Times* (New York: Simon & Schuster, 2018), 55.

3. Sidney M. Milkis, *Theodore Roosevelt, the Progressive Party, and the Transformation of American Democracy* (Lawrence: University Press of Kansas, 2009), 55.

4. Kenneth S. Davis, *FDR: The Beckoning of Destiny, 1882–1928* (New York: Random House, 1971), chaps. 11–17.

5. William E. Leuchtenburg, "The New Deal and the Analogue of War," in *Change and Continuity in Twentieth-Century America*, ed. John Braeman, Robert H. Bremner, and Everett Walters (Columbus: Ohio State University Press, 1964), 81–143.

6. Davis, *FDR*, 613.

7. "The Reminiscences of Robert H. Jackson," Oral History Research Office, Columbia University (1955).

8. Jeff Shesol, *Supreme Power: Franklin Roosevelt vs. the Supreme Court* (New York: W. W. Norton, 2010), 50. In New York, the state supreme court is called the court of appeals.

9. Harold W. Stanley and Richard G. Niemi, *Vital Statistics on American Politics, 2009–2019* (Washington, DC: CQ Press, 2010), 379, 396.

10. The concept of empowering elections is explained in Erwin C. Hargrove and Michael Nelson, *Presidents, Politics, and Policy* (Baltimore: Johns Hopkins University Press, 1984), chap. 3.

11. Donald A. Ritchie, *Electing FDR: The New Deal Campaign of 1932* (Lawrence: University Press of Kansas, 2007), 5.

12. Franklin R. Roosevelt, "Address at Oglethorpe University in Atlanta, Georgia, May 22, 1932," American Presidency Project, https://www.presidency.ucsb.edu/documents/address-oglethorpe-university-atlanta-georgia.

13. Fred I. Greenstein, *The Presidential Difference: Leadership Style from FDR to Clinton* (New York: Free Press, 2000), 19–20.

14. Hargrove and Nelson, *Presidents, Politics, and Policy*.

15. Jonathan Alter, *The Defining Moment: FDR's Hundred Days and the Triumph of Hope* (New York: Simon & Schuster, 2006), 5–6, 82, 221.

16. Eric Rauchway, *Winter War: Hoover, Roosevelt, and the First Clash over the New Deal* (New York: Basic Books, 2018), 190–193.

17. Leuchtenburg, "New Deal and Analogue of War," 103. In 1936 Landon was FDR's Republican opponent in the election.

18. Rauchway, *Winter War*, 5.

19. Franklin D. Roosevelt, "Inaugural Address, March 4, 1933," American Presidency Project, https://www.presidency.ucsb.edu/documents/inaugural-address-8.

20. The classic articulation of the legal realism approach is Benjamin Cardozo, *The Nature of the Judicial Process* (New Haven, CT: Yale University Press, 1921), which includes this statement: "The great tides and currents which engulf the rest of men, do not turn aside in their course, and pass the judges by" (168). On the emergence of the living Constitution theory, see G. Edward White, *The Constitution and the New Deal* (Cambridge, MA: Harvard University Press, 2000).

21. James F. Simon, *FDR and Chief Justice Hughes: The President, the Supreme Court, and the Epic Battle over the New Deal* (New York: Simon & Schuster, 2012), 39–40.

22. The lectures were later published in Charles Evans Hughes, *The Supreme Court of the United States* (Garden City, NY: Garden City Publishing, 1936), 51–53.

23. Merlo J. Pusey, *Charles Evans Hughes*, vol. 2 (New York: Macmillan, 1951), 717.

24. Torbjorn Sirevag, "Rooseveltian Ideas and the 1937 Court Fight: A Neglected Factor," *Historian* 33 (August 1971): 578–595.

25. Burton K. Wheeler, *Yankee from the West* (Garden City, NY: Doubleday, 1952), 330.

26. Joseph Alsop and Turner Catledge, *The 168 Days* (Garden City, NY: Doubleday, Doran, 1938), 16.

27. According to FDR's secretary of labor, Frances Perkins, this did not stop Stone from advising her in 1934 how to draft the Social Security Act so it would

pass the court's muster. "The taxing power of the federal government, my dear," she recalled Stone saying, "the taxing power is sufficient for everything you want and need." As a result, the act provided for Social Security to be funded by a special tax, not from the general revenue. Frances Perkins, *The Roosevelt I Knew* (New York: Harper Colophon, 1964), 286.

28. Robert Dahl, "Decision-Making in a Democracy: The Supreme Court as a National Policy-Maker," *Journal of Public Law* 6 (Fall 1957): 279–295; Richard Funston, "The Supreme Court and Critical Elections," *American Political Science Review* 69 (September 1975): 795–811.

29. For an account of Hughes's presidential candidacy and narrow defeat, see Lewis L. Gould, *The First Modern Clash over Federal Power: Wilson versus Hughes in the Presidential Election of 1916* (Lawrence: University Press of Kansas, 2016).

30. Gould, 71.

31. Hargrove and Nelson, *Presidents, Politics, and Policy*.

32. Arthur Krock, "Tide Sweeps Nation; Democrats Clinch Two-Thirds Rule of the Senate," *New York Times*, November 7, 1934.

33. Michael Kazin, *What It Took to Win: A History of the Democratic Party* (New York: Farrar, Straus & Giroux, 2022), 186.

34. Ira Katznelson, *Fear Itself: The New Deal and the Origins of Our Time* (New York: Liveright, 2013), 287–289.

35. Although Blacks constituted only 3 percent of the voting-age population outside the South, they were concentrated in large industrial states such as Michigan, Illinois, and New York. Two-thirds of Blacks lived in the South, where only about 5 percent of them could vote. John W. Jeffries, *A Third Term for FDR: The Election of 1940* (Lawrence: University Press of Kansas, 2017), 22. In 1936 FDR won an estimated 76 percent of the Black vote. Alonzo L. Hamby, *For the Survival of Democracy: Franklin Roosevelt and the World Crisis of the 1930s* (New York: Free Press, 2004), 324.

36. Michael Nelson, "A Short, Ironic History of American National Bureaucracy," *Journal of Politics* 44 (August 1982): 747–778.

37. Goodwin, *Leadership in Turbulent Times*, 294.

38. These acronyms stood for, respectively, the National Recovery Administration, Civilian Conservation Corps, Civil Works Administration, and Public Works Administration.

39. Arthur M. Schlesinger Jr., *The Coming of the New Deal* (Boston: Houghton Mifflin, 1959), 535.

40. Matthew J. Dickinson, *Bitter Harvest: FDR, Presidential Power and the Growth of the Presidential Branch* (New York: Cambridge University Press, 1997), chap. 2.

41. Joshua Braver, "Court-Packing: An American Tradition," *Boston College Law Review* 61 (2020): 2749–2808. As Braver points out, the geographic rationale for increasing the size of the Supreme Court vanished when justices stopped traveling to help staff the growing number of circuit courts.

42. Gitlow v. New York, 268 U.S. 652 (1925). It and two subsequent cases—

Near v. Minnesota, 274 U.S. 357 (1927), and *Stromberg v. California*, 283 U.S. 359 (1931)—drew on the Fourteenth Amendment's due process clause to apply First Amendment rights to the states. *Powell v. Alabama*, 287 U.S. 45 (1932), took a similar approach to some of the criminal justice provisions of the Bill of Rights. See Barry Cushman, "The Secret Lives of the Four Horsemen," *Virginia Law Review* 83 (April 1997): 559–645.

43. See, for example, Gary L. McDowell, *Curbing the Courts: The Constitution and the Limits of Judicial Power* (Baton Rouge: Louisiana State University Press, 1988), 143–145.

44. Joseph L. Rauh Jr., "An Unabashed Liberal Looks at a Half-Century of the Supreme Court," *North Carolina Law Review* 69 (1990): 213–249.

45. For a thorough account of the appointments of the nine justices, see Henry J. Abraham, *Justices, Presidents, and Senators: A History of Supreme Court Appointments from Washington to Clinton* (Lanham, MD: Rowman & Littlefield, 1999), 126–155.

46. The one Republican-appointed justice to resign under a Democratic president was Charles Evans Hughes, who resigned from the court while Wilson was president in order to run against him in 1916. Drew Pearson and Robert Allen, *The Nine Old Men* (Garden City, NY: Doubleday, Doran, 1936), 321.

47. Burt Solomon, *FDR v. the Constitution: The Court-Packing Fight and the Triumph of Democracy* (New York: Walker, 2009), 60–61.

48. Glendon A. Schubert, "The Study of Judicial Decision-Making as an Aspect of Political Behavior," *American Political Science Review* 52 (December 1958): 1007–1025; Daniel J. Danelski, "The Influence of the Chief Justice in the Decisional Process of the Supreme Court," in *The Federal Judicial System: Readings in Process and Behavior*, ed. Thomas P. Jahnige and Sheldon Goldman (New York: Holt, Rinehart & Winston, 1968), 147–160.

49. C. Herman Pritchett, *The Roosevelt Court: A Study in Judicial Politics and Values, 1937–1947* (New York: Macmillan, 1948), 25.

50. Home Building & Loan v. Blaisdell, 290 U.S. 398 (1934); Nebbia v. New York, 291 U.S. 502 (1934).

51. Peter H. Irons, *The New Deal Lawyers* (Princeton, NJ: Princeton University Press, 1982), 10–13.

52. Shesol, *Supreme Power*, 56–57.

53. Marian C. McKenna, *Franklin Roosevelt and the Great Constitutional War: The Court-Packing Crisis of 1937* (New York: Fordham University Press, 2002), 15, 84. Cummings's main credentials were that, as former chair of the Democratic National Committee, he nominated FDR for president at the 1932 Democratic National Convention. As attorney general, Cummings initially allowed the Justice Department to become a dumping ground for Democratic lawyers that Postmaster General James Farley, the president's patronage boss, sent his way. In the view of government lawyer Thomas Emerson, "The Department of Justice was then at its lowest ebb of any time during the New Deal period in terms of the capacity of its personnel." McKenna, 84.

54. William F. Swindler, *Court and Constitution in the 20th Century: The New Legality, 1932–1968* (Indianapolis: Bobbs-Merrill, 1970), 39.

55. Michael E. Parrish, "The Great Depression, the New Deal, and the American Legal Order," *Washington Law Review* 59 (1984): 723–740.

56. Swindler, *Court and Constitution in the 20th Century*, 5.

57. "Reminiscences of Robert H. Jackson"; Shesol, *Supreme Power*, 40; Dennis J. Hutchinson and David J. Garrow, eds., *The Forgotten Memoir of John Knox: A Year in the Life of a Supreme Court Clerk in FDR's Washington* (Chicago: University of Chicago Press, 2002), 57.

58. The Gold Clause cases were *Norman v. Baltimore & Ohio Railroad*, 294 U.S. 250 (1935); *Nortz v. United States*, 294 U.S. 317; and *Perry v. United States*, 294 U.S. 330 (1935).

59. Panama Refining Co. v. Ryan, 293 U.S. 388 (1935), also known as the Hot Oil case.

60. Harold Ickes, *The Secret Diary of Harold L. Ickes: The First Thousand Days, 1933–1936* (New York: Simon & Schuster, 1953), 274; McKenna, *Franklin Roosevelt and the Great Constitutional War*, 54; William E. Leuchtenburg, *The Supreme Court Reborn: The Constitutional Revolution in the Age of Roosevelt* (New York: Oxford University Press, 1995), 86.

61. Robert H. Jackson, *That Man: An Insider's Portrait of Franklin D. Roosevelt*, ed. John Q. Barrett (New York: Oxford University Press, 2003), 65. The article was Sidney Ratner, "Was the Supreme Court Packed by President Grant?" *Political Science Quarterly* 50 (September 1935): 343–358.

62. Arthur M. Schlesinger Jr., *The Politics of Upheaval* (Boston: Houghton Mifflin, 1960), 258.

CHAPTER 2. TO DO OR NOT TO DO?

1. Perry v. United States, 294 U.S. 330 (1935).

2. Marian C. McKenna, *Franklin Roosevelt and the Great Constitutional War: The Court-Packing Crisis of 1937* (New York: Fordham University Press, 2002), 61.

3. Railroad Retirement Board v. Alton Railroad Co., 295 U.S. 330 (1935).

4. A. L. A. Schechter Poultry Corp. v. United States, 295 U.S. 495 (1935).

5. Louisville Joint Stock Land Bank v. Radford, 295 U.S. 555 (1935). The Fifth Amendment states: "Nor shall private property be taken for public use, without just compensation."

6. Humphrey's Executor v. United States, 295 U.S. 602 (1935).

7. Robert H. Jackson, *That Man: An Insider's Portrait of Franklin D. Roosevelt*, ed. John Q. Barrett (New York: Oxford University Press, 2003), 66.

8. Jeff Shesol, *Supreme Power: Franklin Roosevelt vs. the Supreme Court* (New York: W. W. Norton, 2010), 137.

9. "The Reminiscences of Robert H. Jackson," Oral History Research Office, Columbia University (1960).

10. Myers v. United States, 272 U.S. 52 (1926); Jackson, *That Man*, 19.

11. William E. Leuchtenburg, *The Supreme Court Reborn: The Constitutional Revolution in the Age of Roosevelt* (New York: Oxford University Press, 1995), 92–93.

12. Shesol, *Supreme Power*, 129.

13. Franklin D. Roosevelt, "Press Conference, May 31, 1935," American Presidency Project, https://www.presidency.ucsb.edu/documents/press-conference-23.

14. United States v. Butler, 297 U.S. 1 (1936).

15. Ashwander v. Tennessee Valley Authority, 297 U.S. 288 (1936); Carter v. Carter Coal Co., 296 U.S. 238 (1936).

16. Ashton v. Cameron County Water Improvement District No. 1, 298 U.S. 513 (1936).

17. Alex Badas, "Policy Disagreement and Judicial Legitimacy: Evidence from the 1937 Court-Packing Plan," *Journal of Legal Studies* 48 (June 2019): 377–408.

18. Harold Ickes, *The Secret Diary of Harold L. Ickes: The First Thousand Days, 1933–1936* (New York: Simon & Schuster, 1953), 496. The potential ire of farmers was allayed by the Soil Conservation and Domestic Allotment Act, which restored some of the benefits they had received under the Agricultural Adjustment Act.

19. Morehead v. New York ex rel Tipaldo, 298 U.S. 587 (1936).

20. Arthur M. Schlesinger Jr., *The Politics of Upheaval* (Boston: Houghton Mifflin, 1960), 489.

21. Leuchtenburg, *Supreme Court Reborn*, 92.

22. Leuchtenburg, 83.

23. Author's calculation from table 1 in Stuart S. Nagel, "Court-Curbing Periods in American History," *Vanderbilt Law Review* 18 (March 1965): 926.

24. Tom S. Clark, *The Limits of Judicial Independence* (New York: Cambridge University Press, 2011), 43–52. Clark identifies 1882–1887 and 1906–1911 as previous periods of high court-curbing activity. (I would add 1801–1805, when President Thomas Jefferson took on the courts, and 1866–1869, the post-Civil War years of politically motivated oscillations in the size of the Supreme Court.) Clark also identifies 1975–1982 and 2001–2008 as periods when attempts to limit the Supreme Court came from the political right. As noted in the preface to this book, the late 2010s and the 2020s have witnessed a revival of liberal attacks on the courts.

25. Raymond Moley, *After Seven Years* (New York: Harper & Brothers, 1939), 307; Schlesinger, *Politics of Upheaval*, 491.

26. Schlesinger, *Politics of Upheaval*, 491–492; Leuchtenburg, *Supreme Court Reborn*, 91–92.

27. Ickes, *Secret Diary*, 467–468.

28. This proposal had been a plank in the 1924 Progressive Party platform. Burton Wheeler was the party's vice-presidential candidate, sharing the ticket with presidential nominee Robert M. La Follette of Wisconsin. Robert M. La Follette Jr. succeeded his father in the Senate after he died in 1925.

29. The idea that court packing is wrong was more a consequence than a cause of FDR's failed effort in 1937. See Tara L. Grove, "The Origins (and Fragility) of Judicial Independence," *Vanderbilt Law Review* 71 (2018): 465–545.

30. Article III, section 1, of the US Constitution states that judges' compensation "shall not be diminished during their continuance in office."

31. On this basis, Roosevelt told a January 1936 meeting of the cabinet that "he is not at all averse to the Supreme Court declaring one New Deal statute after another unconstitutional." Ickes, *Secret Diary*, 524.

32. Hadley Cantril and Mildred Strunk, *Public Opinion, 1935–1946* (Princeton, NJ: Princeton University Press, 1951), 148. See also Barry Cushman, "Mr. Dooley and Mr. Gallup: Public Opinion and Constitutional Change in the 1930s," *Buffalo Law Review* 50 (2002): 7–101.

33. George Creel, *Rebel at Large: Recollections of Fifty Crowded Years* (New York: G. P. Putnam's Sons, 1947), 291–292.

34. Leonard Baker, *Back to Back: The Duel between FDR and the Supreme Court* (New York: Macmillan, 1967), 8.

35. Ickes, *Secret Diary*, 705.

36. Richard Tanner Johnson, *Managing the White House: An Intimate Study of the Presidency* (New York: Harper & Row, 1974).

37. Ickes, *Secret Diary*, 705.

38. Independently, another National Recovery Administration lawyer, Jack Scott, worked with Thomas Corcoran on an amendment based on language from the 1787 Constitutional Convention's Virginia Plan, empowering Congress "to legislate in all cases for the general interests of the union." The argument that such language would be immune from misinterpretation, willful or otherwise, by the Supreme Court never persuaded Roosevelt. David E. Kyvig, *Explicit and Authentic Acts: Amending the U.S. Constitution, 1776–1995* (Lawrence: University Press of Kansas, 1996).

39. Joseph Alsop and Turner Catledge, *The 168 Days* (Garden City, NY: Doubleday, Doran, 1938), 20; McKenna, *Franklin Roosevelt and the Great Constitutional War*, 223.

40. Kyvig, *Explicit and Authentic Acts*, 299–303.

41. Carl Brent Swisher, ed., *Selected Papers of Homer Cummings: Attorney General of the United States, 1922–1939* (New York: Charles Scribner's Sons, 1939), 148–149.

42. Ickes, *Secret Diary*, 329–330.

43. Ickes, 495.

44. Introduction to *The Public Papers and Addresses of Franklin D. Roosevelt, 1937: The Constitution Prevails* (New York: Macmillan, 1941), lxi.

45. Cantril and Strunk, *Public Opinion*, 148.

CHAPTER 3. THE 1936 ELECTION: FDR DECIDES NOT TO DECIDE

1. Black voters, historically Republican, swung from three-fourths against FDR in 1932 to three-fourths for him in 1936. Donald A. Ritchie, *Electing FDR: The New Deal Campaign of 1932* (Lawrence: University Press of Kansas, 2007), 189.

2. Arthur M. Schlesinger Jr., *The Politics of Upheaval* (Boston: Houghton Mifflin, 1960), 603.

3. Joseph Alsop and Turner Catledge, *The 168 Days* (Garden City, NY: Double-day, Doran, 1938), 18.

4. William E. Leuchtenburg, *The Supreme Court Reborn: The Constitutional Revolution in the Age of Roosevelt* (New York: Oxford University Press, 1995), 99.

5. Marian C. McKenna, *Franklin Roosevelt and the Great Constitutional War: The Court-Packing Crisis of 1937* (New York: Fordham University Press, 2002), 156.

6. "The Reminiscences of Samuel I. Rosenman," Oral History Research Office, Columbia University (1960).

7. Richard Polenberg, *Reorganizing Roosevelt's Government, 1936–1939: The Controversy over Executive Reorganization* (Cambridge, MA: Harvard University Press, 1966), 7.

8. Polenberg, 15.

9. Louis Brownlow, *A Passion for Anonymity: The Autobiography of Louis Brownlow* (Chicago: University of Chicago Press, 1958), 329.

10. Eleanor Roosevelt, *This I Remember* (New York: Harper, 1949), 167–168.

11. Schlesinger, *Politics of Upheaval*, 540.

12. Schlesinger, 572.

13. Schlesinger, 589.

14. Schlesinger, 611.

15. Gallup's final poll showed Roosevelt with 56 percent of the major-party popular vote, 315 solid electoral votes, and as many as 192 additional electoral votes in states that were too close to call. "Straw Vote Fight Arouses Interest," *Pittsburgh Press*, November 2, 1936, https://news.google.com/newspapers?id=fkYbAAAAI-BAJ&sjid=IU8EAAAAIBAJ&pg=2555,806060&dq=literary-digest&hl=en.

16. George H. Gallup, *The Gallup Poll: Public Opinion, 1935–1971*, vol. 1 (New York: Random House, 1972), 32–33.

17. Dennis J. Hutchinson and David J. Garrow, eds., *The Forgotten Memoir of John Knox: A Year in the Life of a Supreme Court Clerk in FDR's Washington* (Chicago: University of Chicago Press, 2002), 110.

18. Leuchtenburg, *Supreme Court Reborn*, 109.

19. Leuchtenburg, 43; Burt Solomon, *FDR v. the Constitution: The Court-Packing Fight and the Triumph of Democracy* (New York: Walker, 2009), 212.

20. Jeff Shesol, *Supreme Power: Franklin Roosevelt vs. the Supreme Court* (New York: W. W. Norton, 2010), 230.

21. Leonard Baker, *Back to Back: The Duel between FDR and the Supreme Court* (New York: Macmillan, 1967), 124.

22. Rachel Shelden, "Anatomy of a Presidential Campaign from the Supreme Court: John McClean, Levi Woodbury, and the Election of 1848," *Journal of Supreme Court History* 47 (2022), forthcoming.

23. John P. Frank, "Conflict of Interest and U.S. Supreme Court Justices," *American Journal of Comparative Law* 16 (Autumn 1970): 744–761.

24. Carl Schurz et al., *Reminiscences of Carl Schurz*, vol. 2 (New York: McClure, 1907), 172.

25. Noah Feldman, *Scorpions: The Battles and Triumphs of FDR's Great Supreme*

Court Justices (New York: Twelve, 2010), 109, 17, 188-193, 262, 317-319; James L. Moses, "'An Interesting Game of Poker': Franklin D. Roosevelt, William O. Douglas, and the 1944 Vice Presidential Nomination," in *Franklin D. Roosevelt and the Transformation of the Supreme Court*, ed. Stephen K. Smith, William D. Pederson, and Frank J. Williams (Armonk, NY: M. E. Sharpe, 2004), 133-161.

26. Leuchtenburg, *Supreme Court Reborn*, 105.

27. Schlesinger, *Politics of Upheaval*, 489.

28. Kenneth S. Davis, *FDR: The New Deal Years, 1933-1937* (New York: Random House, 1979), 626-627.

29. Shesol, *Supreme Power*, 233.

30. James F. Simon, *FDR and Chief Justice Hughes: The President, the Supreme Court, and the Epic Battle over the New Deal* (New York: Simon & Schuster, 2012), 294.

31. Shesol, *Supreme Power*, 224.

32. Burton K. Wheeler with Paul F. Healy, *Yankee from the West* (Garden City, NY: Doubleday, 1962), 320.

33. "1936 Democratic Party Platform, June 23, 1936," American Presidency Project, https://www.presidency.ucsb.edu/documents/1936-democratic-party-plat form.

34. McKenna, *Franklin Roosevelt and the Great Constitutional War*, 234.

35. Raymond Moley, *After Seven Years* (New York: Harper, 1939), 342.

36. William E. Leuchtenburg, *Franklin D. Roosevelt and the New Deal* (New York: Harper, 1963), 193.

37. Conrad Black, *Franklin Delano Roosevelt: Champion of Freedom* (New York: Public Affairs, 2003), 388.

38. Jean Edward Smith, *FDR* (New York: Random House, 2007), 360-361.

39. Hadley Cantril and Mildred Strunk, *Public Opinion, 1935-1946* (Princeton, NJ: Princeton University Press, 1951), 591-597.

40. William E. Leuchtenburg, "When the People Spoke, What Did They Say? The Election of 1936 and the Ackerman Thesis," *Yale Law Journal* 108 (1999): 2077-2114.

41. Donald Grier Stephenson, *Campaigns and the Court: The U.S. Supreme Court in Presidential Elections* (New York: Columbia University Press, 1999), 151-152.

42. Leuchtenburg, "When the People Spoke, What Did They Say?"

43. James T. Patterson, *Congressional Conservatism and the New Deal* (Lexington: University of Kentucky Press, 1967), 81-82.

44. Rafael Gely and Pablo T. Spiller, "The Political Economy of Supreme Court Constitutional Decisions: The Case of Roosevelt's Court-Packing Plan," *International Review of Law and Economics* 12 (1992): 45-67.

45. James L. Sundquist, *Dynamics of the Party System: Alignment and Realignment of Political Parties in the United States*, rev. ed. (Washington, DC: Brookings Institution, 1983), chap. 10; Robert S. Erikson and Kent L. Tedin, "The 1928-1936 Partisan Realignment: The Case for the Conversion Hypothesis," *American Political Science Review* 75 (December 1981): 951-962.

46. Kristi Andersen, *The Creation of a Democratic Majority: 1928–1936* (Chicago: University of Chicago Press, 1978).

47. James MacGregor Burns, *Roosevelt: The Lion and the Fox, 1882–1940* (New York: Harcourt, 1956), chap. 14.

48. Davis, *FDR*, 633.

49. Harold Ickes, *The Secret Diary of Harold L. Ickes: The First Thousand Days, 1933–1936* (New York: Simon & Schuster, 1953), 602.

50. Introduction to *The Public Papers and Addresses of Franklin D. Roosevelt, 1937: The Constitution Prevails* (New York: Macmillan, 1941), lx.

51. Warner W. Gardner, "Memories of the 1937 Constitutional Revolution, Part I," *Green Bag* 22 (Spring 2019): 219–233.

52. Shesol, *Supreme Power*, 243.

53. Schlesinger, *Politics of Upheaval*, 513.

54. Gallup, *Gallup Poll*, 41. The polls were taken throughout 1935 and 1936.

55. "Reminiscences of Samuel I. Rosenman."

56. Robert Dallek, *Franklin D. Roosevelt: A Political Life* (New York: Viking, 2017), 266.

57. Polenberg, *Reorganizing Roosevelt's Government*, chap. 1.

58. Ickes, *Secret Diary*, 705.

59. Leuchtenburg, *Supreme Court Reborn*, 117.

60. Homer Cummings and Carl McFarland, *Federal Justice: Chapters in the History of Justice and the Federal Executive* (New York: Macmillan, 1937), 531.

61. Leuchtenburg, *Supreme Court Reborn*, 120.

62. Shesol, *Supreme Power*, 252.

63. Leuchtenburg, *Supreme Court Reborn*, 115.

64. George Creel, "Roosevelt's Plans and Purposes," *Collier's*, December 26, 1936. See also George Creel, *Rebel at Large: Recollections of Fifty Crowded Years* (New York: G. P. Putnam's Sons, 1947), 292–294.

65. Drew Pearson and Robert Allen, *The Nine Old Men* (Garden City, NY: Doubleday, Doran, 1936).

66. Leuchtenburg, *Supreme Court Reborn*, 121.

67. McKenna, *Franklin Roosevelt and the Great Constitutional War*, 254.

68. Shesol, *Supreme Power*, 261.

69. William Howard Taft, *Popular Government: Its Essence, Its Permanence and Its Perils* (New Haven, CT: Yale University Press, 1912), 158–160.

70. Shesol, *Supreme Power*, 261.

71. Burns, *Roosevelt*, 296.

72. Richard Tanner Johnson, *Managing the White House: An Intimate Study of the Presidency* (New York: Harper & Row, 1974).

73. For a list of proposals, see Gely and Spiller, "Political Economy of Supreme Court Constitutional Decisions," 58–59.

74. Alsop and Catledge, *The 168 Days*, 36–37; McKenna, *Franklin Roosevelt and the Great Constitutional War*, 250.

CHAPTER 4. THE PRESIDENT PROPOSES

1. Calculated from data in James T. Patterson, *Congressional Conservatism and the New Deal* (Lexington: University of Kentucky Press, 1967), 81–82.

2. In addition, the poll, conducted November 6–11, 1936, found that 35 percent of all voters, including 32 percent of Democrats, hoped FDR's second-term direction would be "about the same as his first [term]." George H. Gallup, *The Gallup Poll: Public Opinion, 1935–1971*, vol. 1 (New York: Random House, 1972), 41.

3. Franklin D. Roosevelt, "Annual Message to Congress, January 6, 1937," American Presidency Project, https://www.presidency.ucsb.edu/documents/annual-message-congress-1.

4. Samuel I. Rosenman, *Working with Roosevelt* (New York: Harper & Brothers, 1952), 141.

5. Roosevelt, "Annual Message to Congress, January 6, 1937."

6. "Summary of the Report of the Committee on Administrative Management," January 12, 1937, American Presidency Project, https://www.presidency.ucsb.edu/documents/summary-the-report-the-committee-administrative-management. For the complete report, see President's Committee on Administrative Management, *Report of the Committee with Studies of Administrative Management in the Federal Government* (Washington, DC: US Government Printing Office, 1937).

7. Peri E. Arnold, *Making the Managerial Presidency: Comprehensive Reorganization Planning, 1905–1980* (Princeton, NJ: Princeton University Press, 1986), 107–108.

8. Sidney M. Milkis, *The President and the Parties: The Transformation of the American Party System since the New Deal* (New York: Oxford University Press, 1993), 118.

9. Kenneth S. Davis, *FDR: Into the Storm, 1937–1940* (New York: Random House, 1993), 35.

10. William E. Leuchtenburg, *Franklin D. Roosevelt and the New Deal* (New York: Harper, 1963), 378; Joseph P. Harris, "The Progress of Administrative Reorganization in the Seventy-Fifth Congress," *American Political Science Review* 21 (October 1937): 862–870. Wallace was right to think that Ickes was out to claim the Forest Service. See, for example, Harold Ickes, *The Secret Diary of Harold L. Ickes: The Inside Struggle, 1936–1939* (New York: Simon & Schuster, 1954), 23, 43.

11. Milkis, *President and the Parties*, 121.

12. James MacGregor Burns, *Roosevelt: The Lion and the Fox, 1882–1940* (New York: Harcourt, 1956), 344.

13. Richard Polenberg, *Reorganizing Roosevelt's Government, 1936–1939: The Controversy over Executive Reorganization* (Cambridge, MA: Harvard University Press, 1966), chaps. 4, 5.

14. Polenberg, 31.

15. Ickes, *Secret Diary*, 152.

16. Franklin D. Roosevelt, "January 20, 1937: Second Inaugural Address," Miller Center, University of Virginia, https://millercenter.org/the-presidency/presidential-speeches/january-20-1937-second-inaugural-address.

17. Robert H. Jackson, *The Struggle for Judicial Supremacy: A Study of a Crisis in American Power* (New York: Knopf, 1941), 321.

18. Jeff Shesol, *Supreme Power: Franklin Roosevelt vs. the Supreme Court* (New York: W. W. Norton, 2010), 264-265. Unknown to Roosevelt or anyone else outside the Supreme Court until the decision was announced on March 29, 1937, on December 19, 1936, Roberts reversed course and voted with Justices Cardozo, Brandeis, and Hughes to uphold a Washington State minimum wage law for women (*West Coast Hotel Co. v. Parrish*, 300 U.S. 379 [1937]). Because Justice Stone was absent due to illness, the vote was four to four. The case was held over until Stone could return and cast the decisive vote. Roberts's "switch" is discussed in chapter 5 of this volume.

19. James A. Farley, *Jim Farley's Story: The Roosevelt Years* (New York: McGraw-Hill, 1948), 73; William E. Leuchtenburg, *The Supreme Court Reborn: The Constitutional Revolution in the Age of Roosevelt* (New York: Oxford University Press, 1995), 126.

20. Jackson, *Struggle for Judicial Supremacy*, 181.

21. Richard J. Ellis, *The Development of the American Presidency*, 2nd ed. (New York: Routledge, 2017), 506.

22. "The Reminiscences of Robert H. Jackson," Oral History Research Office, Columbia University (1955).

23. For example, in a Gallup poll conducted in September 1935, only 31 percent favored "limiting the power of the Supreme Court to declare acts of Congress unconstitutional," compared with 56 percent opposed. When the same question was asked in November 1936, the margin was 41 percent in favor and 59 percent opposed. Gallup, *Gallup Poll*, 2, 43.

24. Leonard Baker, *Back to Back: The Duel between FDR and the Supreme Court* (New York: Macmillan, 1967), chap. 8.

25. David E. Kyvig, "The Road Not Taken: FDR, the Supreme Court, and Constitutional Amendment," *Political Science Quarterly* 104 (1989): 463-481; Bruce Ackerman, *We the People 2: Transformations* (Cambridge, MA: Harvard University Press, 1998), 338.

26. Merlo J. Pusey, *Charles Evans Hughes*, vol. 2 (New York: Macmillan, 1951), 750.

27. Shesol, *Supreme Power*, 286.

28. Shesol, 287.

29. Rosenman, *Working with Roosevelt*, 247.

30. In a February 9, 1937, letter to Harvard law professor Felix Frankfurter, Roosevelt claimed that "the chance of a two-thirds vote in this session [of Congress] was about fifty-fifty," with ratification by enough state legislatures unlikely before the 1940 election. Max Freedman, ed., *Roosevelt and Frankfurter: Their Correspondence, 1928-1945* (Boston: Little, Brown, 1967), 381-382. "Give me ten million dollars and I can prevent any amendment to the Constitution from being ratified," FDR told others. Jean Edward Smith, *FDR* (New York: Random House, 2008), 381.

31. Joseph Alsop and Turner Catledge, *The 168 Days* (Garden City, NY: Doubleday, Doran, 1938), 67.

32. Rayburn and Bankhead squelched subsequent talk about a discharge petition that would take the bill out of the Judiciary Committee and bring it directly to the floor of the House. Circumventing committees was not a practice they wanted to encourage. Alsop and Catledge, *The 168 Days*, 200.

33. Frank Freidel, *Franklin D. Roosevelt: A Rendezvous with Destiny* (Boston: Little, Brown, 1990), 229.

34. Alsop and Catledge, *The 168 Days*, 69.

35. "The Three Hundred and Forty-Second Press Conference, February 5, 1937," in *The Public Papers and Addresses of Franklin D. Roosevelt, 1937: The Constitution Prevails* (New York: Macmillan, 1941), 35.

36. Shesol, *Supreme Power*, 67.

37. Introduction to *Public Papers and Addresses of Franklin D. Roosevelt, 1937.*

38. *Public Papers and Addresses of Franklin D. Roosevelt, 1937*, 42.

39. David J. Garrow, "Mental Decrepitude on the U.S. Supreme Court," *University of Chicago Law Review* 67 (2000): 995–1087.

40. Rosenman, *Working with Roosevelt*, 247.

41. Gallup, *Gallup Poll*, 50, 57.

42. Shesol, *Supreme Power*, 312.

43. The single exception was his proposal in January 1935 that the United States join the World Court.

44. Virtually every contemporary and subsequent account of the court-packing fight acknowledges that Roosevelt "had promised the next opening on the bench to Robinson" and "could hardly avoid choosing the majority leader without a Senate uprising." Leuchtenburg, *Supreme Court Reborn*, 145. As late as May 24, Roosevelt confirmed to Robert Jackson that he had made that promise to Robinson. Robert H. Jackson, *That Man: An Insider's Portrait of Franklin D. Roosevelt*, ed. John Q. Barrett (New York: Oxford University Press, 2003), 53.

45. Ickes, *Secret Diary*, 153. Concerns that court packing was a backhanded attempt to advance civil rights were widespread among southern Democrats. Patterson, *Congressional Conservatism and the New Deal*, 97.

46. Burt Solomon, *FDR v. the Constitution: The Court-Packing Fight and the Triumph of Democracy* (New York: Walker, 2009), 109.

47. Robert Shogan, *Backlash: The Killing of the New Deal* (Chicago: Ivan R. Dee, 2006), 128.

48. Shesol, *Supreme Power*, 310.

49. Gregory A. Caldeira, "FDR's Court-Packing Plan in the Court of Public Opinion" (unpublished paper, Ohio State University, August 2004), 19–20. The independent progressives Wheeler won over were Gerald Nye and Lynn Frazier of North Dakota and Henrik Shipstead of Minnesota. Hiram Johnson of California and William Borah of Idaho were already opposed. Marian C. McKenna, *Franklin Roosevelt and the Great Constitutional War: The Court-Packing Crisis of 1937* (New York: Fordham University Press, 2002).

50. Stephen R. Alton, "Loyal Lieutenant, Able Advocate: The Role of Robert H. Jackson in Franklin D. Roosevelt's Battle with the Supreme Court," *William and Mary Bill of Rights Journal* 5 (May 1997): 527–618. The case was *De Jonge v. Oregon*, 299 U.S. 353 (1937).

51. Patterson, *Congressional Conservatism and the New Deal*, 116.

52. Barry A. Crouch, "Dennis Chavez and Roosevelt's 'Court-Packing' Plan," *New Mexico Historical Review* 42 (1967): 261–280.

53. Harold Ickes, *The Secret Diary of Harold L. Ickes: The First Thousand Days, 1933–1936* (New York: Simon & Schuster, 1953), 363–364.

54. Burton K. Wheeler with Paul F. Healy, *Yankee from the West* (Garden City, NY: Doubleday, 1962), 323.

55. McKenna, *Franklin Roosevelt and the Great Constitutional War*, 303–304.

56. According to the Gallup poll, those who supported Roosevelt's court plan were never in the majority. When Gallup changed the question in late April from "Are you in favor of President Roosevelt's plan to reorganize the Supreme Court?" to "Should Congress pass President Roosevelt's Supreme Court plan?" the margin of disapproval was unchanged from the first poll in February: 47 percent in favor, 53 percent opposed. Gallup, *Gallup Poll*, 53, 54, 55, 57, 58. In polls taken in May and June, opposition rose to 60 percent. Hadley Cantril and Mildred Strunk, *Public Opinion, 1935–1946* (Princeton, NJ: Princeton University Press, 1951), 150.

57. Farley, *Jim Farley's Story*, 73–74; Patterson, *Congressional Conservatism and the New Deal*, 121.

58. For a detailed discussion of one undecided senator's thinking, see Crouch, "Dennis Chavez and Roosevelt's 'Court-Packing' Plan." Like other Democrats, Chavez was torn between loyalty to Roosevelt, whose support had been helpful in winning his Senate seat in 1934, and the combination of opposition mail, bar association hostility, and critical newspaper editorials in his home state.

59. Solomon, *FDR v. the Constitution*, 126–127.

60. McKenna, *Franklin Roosevelt and the Great Constitutional War*, 324.

61. Shesol, *Supreme Power*, 85, 303.

CHAPTER 5. THE SENATE DISPOSES

1. Jeff Shesol, *Supreme Power: Franklin Roosevelt vs. the Supreme Court* (New York: W. W. Norton, 2010), 351.

2. Joseph Alsop and Turner Catledge, *The 168 Days* (Garden City, NY: Doubleday, Doran, 1938), 108.

3. Robert H. Jackson, *That Man: An Insider's Portrait of Franklin D. Roosevelt*, ed. John Q. Barrett (New York: Oxford University Press, 2003), 51.

4. Robert H. Jackson, *The Struggle for Judicial Supremacy: A Study of a Crisis in American Power* (New York: Knopf, 1941), 189.

5. Samuel Kernell, *Going Public: New Strategies of Presidential Leadership*, 4th ed. (Washington, DC: CQ Press, 2007), 24, 134.

6. "The Reminiscences of Robert H. Jackson," Oral History Research Office, Columbia University (1955).

7. Franklin D. Roosevelt, "Address at the Democratic Victory Dinner, Washington DC, March 4, 1937," American Presidency Project, https://www.presidency.ucsb.edu/documents/address-the-democratic-victory-dinner-washington-dc; Burt Solomon, *FDR v. the Constitution: The Court-Packing Fight and the Triumph of Democracy* (New York: Walker, 2009), 130.

8. Franklin D. Roosevelt, "March 9, 1937: Fireside Chat 9: On Court-Packing," Miller Center, University of Virginia, https://millercenter.org/the-presidency/presidential-speeches/march-9-1937-fireside-chat-9-court-packing. In an apt comparison with Roosevelt's "three-horse" metaphor, Donovan Bisbee wrote, "Like Plato's charioteer, the American people are locked in a struggle to control the renegade horse and control its immoral appetites, lest they be dragged down." Donovan Bisbee, "Driving the Three-Horse Team of Government: FDR's Judiciary Fireside Chat," *Rhetoric and Public Affairs* 3 (Fall 2018): 481–521.

9. Hadley Cantril and Mildred Strunk, *Public Opinion, 1935–1946* (Princeton, NJ: Princeton University Press, 1951), 150.

10. Lawrence W. Levine and Cornelia R. Levine, *The People and the President: America's Conversation with FDR* (Boston: Beacon Press, 2002), 180, 183, 187.

11. Gregory A. Caldeira, "Public Opinion and the U.S. Supreme Court: FDR's Court-Packing Plan," *American Political Science Review* 81 (December 1987): 1139–1153.

12. James T. Patterson, *Congressional Conservatism and the New Deal* (Lexington: University of Kentucky Press, 1967), 88.

13. James A. Farley, *Jim Farley's Story: The Roosevelt Years* (New York: McGraw-Hill, 1948), 79.

14. "The people are with me" was Roosevelt's recurring refrain, according to Alsop and Catledge, *The 168 Days*.

15. Leonard Baker, *Back to Back: The Duel between FDR and the Supreme Court* (New York: Macmillan, 1967), 150; Marian C. McKenna, *Franklin Roosevelt and the Great Constitutional War: The Court-Packing Crisis of 1937* (New York: Fordham University Press, 2002), 358.

16. Shesol, *Supreme Power*, 385.

17. William F. Swindler, *Court and Constitution in the 20th Century: The New Legality, 1932–1968* (Indianapolis: Bobbs-Merrill, 1970), 71.

18. Jackson, *Struggle for Judicial Supremacy*, 191.

19. Alsop and Catledge, *The 168 Days*, 115–119.

20. Even before it was declared unconstitutional, the act was unpopular. In an October 1935 Gallup poll, the 41 percent who favored it were outnumbered by the 59 percent who opposed it. George H. Gallup, *The Gallup Poll: Public Opinion, 1935–1971*, vol. 1 (New York: Random House, 1972).

21. William E. Leuchtenburg, *The Supreme Court Reborn: The Constitutional Revolution in the Age of Roosevelt* (New York: Oxford University Press, 1995), 128–129.

22. Michael Kazin, *What It Takes to Win: A History of the Democratic Party* (New York: Farrar, Straus & Giroux, 2022), 175.

23. Joseph P. Lash, *Dealers and Dreamers: New Look at the New Deal* (New York: Doubleday, 1988), 310.

24. Robert Shogan, *Backlash: The Killing of the New Deal* (Chicago: Ivan R. Dee, 2006), 138, 177-178; Farley, *Jim Farley's Story*, 84-86. Garner's departure infuriated Roosevelt.

25. Jean Edward Smith, *FDR* (New York: Random House, 2008), 395.

26. "Reminiscences of Robert H. Jackson."

27. Shesol, *Supreme Power*, 359-366.

28. Baker, *Back to Back*, 153-155.

29. Burton K. Wheeler, *Yankee from the West* (Garden City, NY: Doubleday, 1952), 330.

30. "Text of Hughes Letter," *New York Times*, March 23, 1937.

31. Merlo J. Pusey, *The Supreme Court Crisis* (New York: Macmillan, 1937), 15; Shesol, *Supreme Power*, 394-395.

32. McKenna, *Franklin Roosevelt and the Great Constitutional War*, 379.

33. Harold Ickes, *The Secret Diary of Harold L. Ickes: The Inside Struggle, 1936-1939* (New York: Simon & Schuster, 1954), 145.

34. Max Freedman, ed., *Roosevelt and Frankfurter: Their Correspondence, 1928-1945* (Boston: Little, Brown, 1967), 392.

35. Stone disliked the court-packing plan and said in February that he had "no doubt the Court situation would have righted itself if the president could have possessed himself in patience for a reasonable time." He suggested in April that a constitutional amendment compelling justices to retire by age seventy-five "could be promptly passed and would solve all our troubles." Alphaeus Thomas Mason, "Harlan Fiske Stone and FDR's Court Plan," *Yale Law Journal* 6 (June-July 1952): 791-817. Although none of the justices approved of the court bill, if Hughes had consulted all of them before releasing his letter, some might have objected to his intervention in the congressional debate or, at a minimum, argued about the letter's wording.

36. William G. Ross, *The Chief Justiceship of Charles Evans Hughes, 1930-1941* (Columbia: University of South Carolina Press, 2007), 118.

37. West Coast Hotel Co. v. Parrish, 300 U.S. 379 (1937).

38. The decision explicitly overturned the court's fourteen-year-old ruling in *Adkins v. Children's Hospital*, 261 U.S. 525 (1923), which had overturned a minimum wage law in the District of Columbia. But, perhaps to avoid embarrassing Roberts, it did not explicitly overturn *Tipaldo*. Never before had the Supreme Court overturned one of its own precedents so quickly.

39. Dennis J. Hutchinson and David J. Garrow, eds., *The Forgotten Memoir of John Knox: A Year in the Life of a Supreme Court Clerk in FDR's Washington* (Chicago: University of Chicago Press, 2002), 247. The most important National Labor Relations Act case was *National Labor Relations Board v. Jones and Laughlin Steel Corporation*, 301 U.S. 1 (1937). The major Social Security Act cases were *Steward Machine Co. v. Davis*, 301 U.S. 548 (1937), and *Helvering et al. v. Davis*, 301 U.S. 619 (1937).

40. Caldeira, "Public Opinion and the U.S. Supreme Court." Frank V. Cantwell tracked a fourteen-point decline in support for the court bill in roughly the

same period. Frank V. Cantwell, "Public Opinion and the Legislative Process," *American Political Science Review* 11 (October 1946): 924–935.

41. Franklin D. Roosevelt, "Excerpts from the Press Conference, April 13, 1937," American Presidency Project, https://www.presidency.ucsb.edu/documents/excerpts-from-the-press-conference-120.

42. Farley, *Jim Farley's Story*, 79.

43. Jackson, *That Man*, 3.

44. Freedman, *Roosevelt and Frankfurter*, 392.

45. It is unclear who came up with the phrase "a switch in time that saved nine." For different views, see, for example, Shesol, *Supreme Power*, 590; and Donald A. Ritchie, *Reporting from Washington: The History of the Washington Press Corps* (New York: Oxford University Press, 2005), 95–96. Considering the familiarity of the aphorism "a stitch in time saves nine," it is possible that a number of people independently thought of the variation to describe Roberts's decision and its effect on the court plan.

46. Nebbia v. New York, 291 U.S. 502 (1934).

47. For an overview of the debate, see the four articles in Alan Brinkley, ed., "AHR Forum: The Debate over the Constitutional Revolution of 1937," *American Historical Review* 110 (October 2005): 1046–1115. See the bibliographic essay in this volume for a more complete list of books and articles.

48. John W. Chambers points out that there is no proof Roberts voted to hear the case, and even if he did, this did not necessarily predict his vote. John W. Chambers, "The Big Switch: Justice Roberts and the Minimum-Wage Case," *Labor History* 10 (1969): 44–73.

49. Introduction to *The Public Papers and Addresses of Franklin D. Roosevelt, 1937: The Constitution Prevails* (New York: Macmillan, 1941), lxix. It is possible that FDR's landslide reelection and his court bill contributed to Roberts's liberal votes in subsequent cases in 1937, most of which were argued after the bill's introduction. Tom S. Clark, *The Limits of Judicial Independence* (New York: Cambridge University Press, 2011), 197.

50. Baker, *Back to Back*, 124.

51. Owen J. Roberts, "Now Is the Time: Fortifying the Supreme Court's Independence," *American Bar Association Journal* 35 (January 1949): 1–4.

52. Merlo J. Pusey, *Charles Evans Hughes*, vol. 2 (New York: Macmillan, 1951), 757.

53. Alsop and Catledge, *The 168 Days*, 153.

54. Stephen R. Alton, "Loyal Lieutenant, Able Advocate: The Role of Robert H. Jackson in Franklin D. Roosevelt's Battle with the Supreme Court," *William and Mary Bill of Rights Journal* 5 (May 1997): 527–618.

55. Kenneth S. Davis, *FDR: Into the Storm, 1937–1940* (New York: Random House, 1993), 66–67.

56. McKenna, *Franklin Roosevelt and the Great Constitutional War*, 445–446.

57. Barry Cushman, "Court-Packing and Compromise," *Constitutional Commentary* 29 (2013): 1–30.

58. Roberts's shift was "sudden and temporary." After *Parrish*, he voted with the liberals for the rest of the term, but he did not do so during his remaining eight years on the Supreme Court. Daniel E. Ho and Kevin M. Quinn, "Did a Switch in Time Save Nine?" *Journal of Legal Analysis* 2 (Spring 2010): 69–113. Roberts wrote fifty-three dissents from liberal decisions in 1944–1945 alone. Solomon, *FDR v. the Constitution*, 270. See also Cushman, "Court-Packing and Compromise."

59. Committee on the Judiciary, US Senate, "Reorganization of the Federal Judiciary: Adverse Report," June 14, 1937, https://reason.com/wp-content/up loads/2020/10/Senate-Judiciary-Committee-Report-on-1937-Court-Packing-Le gislation.pdf.

60. Shesol, *Supreme Power*, 470.

61. Baker, *Back to Back*, 249–250.

62. Ickes, *Secret Diary*, 153.

63. James MacGregor Burns, *Roosevelt: The Lion and the Fox, 1882–1940* (New York: Harcourt, 1956), 307.

64. Alsop and Catledge, *The 168 Days*, 248–252.

65. Davis, *FDR*, 95.

66. Alsop and Catledge, *The 168 Days*, 289.

67. Baker, *Back to Back*, 273.

68. Kazin, *What It Takes to Win*, 187; William E. Leuchtenburg, *Franklin D. Roosevelt and the New Deal* (New York: Harper, 1963), 252.

69. Peri E. Arnold, *Making the Managerial Presidency: Comprehensive Reorganization Planning, 1905–1980* (Princeton, NJ: Princeton University Press, 1986), 108.

70. Farley, *Jim Farley's Story*, 95.

CHAPTER 6. DID FDR SUCCEED?

1. Richard E. Neustadt, *Presidential Power* (New York: John Wiley & Sons, 1960), 33.

2. Franklin D. Roosevelt, "Address at the Democratic Victory Dinner, Washington DC, March 4, 1937," American Presidency Project, https://www.presidency.ucsb.edu/documents/address-the-democratic-victory-dinner-washington-dc.

3. "The Reminiscences of Samuel I. Rosenman," Oral History Research Office, Columbia University (1960); Donald Richberg, *My Hero* (New York: G. P. Putnam's Sons, 1954), 226.

4. Introduction to *The Public Papers and Addresses of Franklin D. Roosevelt, 1937: The Constitution Prevails* (New York: Macmillan, 1941), lxvi. For an argument that Roosevelt was right to claim victory, see Jamie L. Carson and Benjamin A. Kleinerman, "A Switch in Time Saves Nine: Institutions, Strategic Actors, and FDR's Court-Packing Plan," *Public Choice* 113 (December 2002): 301–324.

5. West Coast Hotel Co. v. Parrish, 300 U.S. 379 (1937).

6. William E. Leuchtenburg, *The Supreme Court Reborn: The Constitutional Revolution in the Age of Roosevelt* (New York: Oxford University Press, 1995), 154, 233.

7. Nebbia v. New York, 292 U.S. 491 (1934).

8. In that limited sense, I agree with "internalist" legal scholars such as Barry Cushman and G. Edward White that Roberts's votes in *Parrish* and other 1937 cases did not come entirely out of the blue. See, for example, Barry Cushman, *Rethinking the New Deal: The Structure of a Constitutional Revolution* (New York: Oxford University Press, 1998); G. Edward White, *The Constitution and the New Deal* (Cambridge, MA: Harvard University Press, 2000).

9. Salaries had been frozen at $20,000 per year since 1926, considerably less than the norm for partners in major law firms.

10. William F. Swindler, *Court and Constitution in the 20th Century: The New Legality, 1932–1968* (Indianapolis: Bobbs-Merrill, 1970), 72.

11. Leonard Baker, *Back to Back: The Duel between FDR and the Supreme Court* (New York: Macmillan, 1967), 8.

12. Calculated from data in Paul M. Collins Jr. and Matthew Eshbaugh-Soha, *The President and the Supreme Court: Going Public on Judicial Decisions from Washington to Trump* (New York: Cambridge University Press, 2019), 192, 200.

13. The average rises to fifty-one if Stone is included at the time of his elevation to chief justice. He was fifty-two when first appointed to the Supreme Court.

14. John R. Schmidhauser, "The Justices of the Supreme Court: A Collective Portrait," *Midwest Journal of Political Science* 1 (February 1959): 1–57.

15. Congress removed the three-judge requirement for issuing injunctions in 1976.

16. Marian C. McKenna, *Franklin Roosevelt and the Great Constitutional War: The Court-Packing Crisis of 1937* (New York: Fordham University Press, 2002), 538.

17. Rexford G. Tugwell, *The Democratic Roosevelt* (Garden City, NY: Doubleday, 1957), 407.

18. Leuchtenburg, *Supreme Court Reborn*, chap. 9.

19. Adam Liptak, "A Transformative Term at the Most Conservative Supreme Court in Nearly a Century," *New York Times*, July 1, 2022. Liptak drew his data from Washington University Law School's Supreme Court Database, http://scdb.wustl.edu/.

20. Franklin D. Roosevelt, "Letter on the Reorganization Bill, March 29, 1938," American Presidency Project, https://www.presidency.ucsb.edu/documents/letter-the-reorganization-bill.

21. Wayne S. Cole, *Roosevelt and the Isolationists, 1932–1945* (Lincoln: University of Nebraska Press, 1983), 221–222.

22. Richard Polenberg, *Reorganizing Roosevelt's Government, 1936–1939* (Cambridge, MA: Harvard University Press, 1966), 165.

23. John P. Burke, *The Institutional Presidency: Organizing and Managing the White House from FDR to Clinton*, 2nd ed. (Baltimore: Johns Hopkins University Press, 2000), 11.

24. Burke, 13.

25. The Bureau of the Budget became the Office of Management and Budget in 1970.

26. Richard E. Neustadt, "Presidency and Legislation: The Growth of Central Clearance," *American Political Science Review* 48 (September 1954): 641–671.

27. Herbert Emmerich, *Federal Organization and Administrative Management* (University: University of Alabama Press, 1971), 57.

28. For a list of modest exceptions, see Kenneth S. Davis, *FDR: Into the Storm, 1937–1940* (New York: Random House, 1993), 100.

29. William E. Leuchtenburg, *Franklin D. Roosevelt and the New Deal* (New York: Harper, 1963), 263.

30. Ronald L. Feinman, *The Twilight of Progressivism: The Western Republican Senators and the New Deal* (Baltimore: Johns Hopkins University Press, 1981), chap. 8.

31. James T. Patterson, *Congressional Conservatism and the New Deal: The Growth of the Conservative Coalition in Congress, 1933–1939* (Lexington: University of Kentucky Press, 1967).

32. Sidney M. Milkis, *The President and the Parties: The Transformation of the American Party System since the New Deal* (New York: Oxford University Press, 1993).

33. "Reminiscences of Samuel I. Rosenman."

34. Samuel I. Rosenman, *Working with Roosevelt* (New York: Harper & Brothers, 1952), 276.

35. James A. Farley, *Jim Farley's Story: The Roosevelt Years* (New York: McGraw-Hill, 1948), 120.

36. Franklin D. Roosevelt, "Address at Gainesville, Georgia, March 23, 1938," American Presidency Project, https://www.presidency.ucsb.edu/documents/address-gainesville-georgia.

37. Hadley Cantril and Mildred Strunk, *Public Opinion, 1935–1946* (Princeton, NJ: Princeton University Press, 1951), 576.

38. "Historical Rankings of the Presidents," Wikipedia https://en.wikipedia.org/wiki/Historical_rankings_of_presidents_of_the_United_States.

39. Franklin D. Roosevelt, "Excerpts from the Press Conference, December 28, 1943," American Presidency Project, https://www.presidency.ucsb.edu/documents/excerpts-from-the-press-conference-8.

40. William Shakespeare, *Macbeth*, act I, scene 7, ll. 25–28.

41. As Lee Epstein and colleagues reported, based on a survey of public opinion conducted in October 2020, "a far smaller percentage of Americans today favor plans to enlarge the Court than in the 1930s"—just 26 percent. Lee Epstein, James L. Gibson, and Michael J. Nelson, "Public Response to Proposals to Reform the Supreme Court," October 9, 2020, https://static1.squarespace.com/static/60188505fb790b33c3d33a61/t/604af3977ee0a433fbaeea34/1615524760442/CourtReformSurvey.pdf.

42. "The Reminiscences of Robert H. Jackson," Oral History Research Office, Columbia University (1955).

43. Introduction to *Public Papers and Addresses of Franklin D. Roosevelt, 1937*, lviii–lix.

44. "Reminiscences of Robert H. Jackson."

BIBLIOGRAPHIC ESSAY

Franklin D. Roosevelt's campaign to pack the Supreme Court has been the subject of multiple fine books. These include Joseph Alsop and Turner Catledge, *The 168 Days* (Garden City, NY: Doubleday, Doran, 1938); Leonard Baker, *Back to Back: The Duel between FDR and the Supreme Court* (New York: Macmillan, 1967); William E. Leuchtenburg, *The Supreme Court Reborn: The Constitutional Revolution in the Age of Roosevelt* (New York: Oxford University Press, 1995); Bruce Ackerman, *We the People 2: Transformations* (Cambridge, MA: Harvard University Press, 1998); Marian C. McKenna, *Franklin Roosevelt and the Great Constitutional War: The Court-Packing Crisis of 1937* (New York: Fordham University Press, 2002); Robert Shogan, *Backlash: The Killing of the New Deal* (Chicago: Ivan R. Dee, 2006); Burt Solomon, *FDR v. the Constitution: The Court-Packing Fight and the Triumph of Democracy* (New York: Walker, 2009); Jeff Shesol, *Supreme Power: Franklin Roosevelt vs. the Supreme Court* (New York: W. W. Norton, 2010); and James F. Simon, *FDR and Chief Justice Hughes: The President, the Supreme Court, and the Epic Battle over the New Deal* (New York: Simon & Schuster, 2012).

Scholarly articles have also contributed to the rich literature on the subject, including Frank V. Cantwell, "Public Opinion and the Legislative Process," *American Political Science Review* 11 (October 1946): 924–935; Alphaeus Thomas Mason, "Harlan Fiske Stone and FDR's Court Plan," *Yale Law Journal* 6 (June–July 1952): 791–817; John W. Chambers, "The Big Switch: Justice Roberts and the Minimum-Wage Case," *Labor History* 10 (1969): 44–73; Gregory A. Caldeira, "Public Opinion and the U.S. Supreme Court: FDR's Court-Packing Plan," *American Political Science Review* 81 (December 1987): 1139–1153; Glendon A. Schubert, "The Study of Judicial Decision-Making as an Aspect of Political Behavior," *American Political Science Review* 52 (December 1958): 1007–1025; Michael Nelson, "The President and the Court: Reinterpreting the Court-Packing Episode of 1937," *Political Science Quarterly* 103 (Summer 1988): 267–293; Rafael Gely and Pablo T. Spiller, "The Political Economy of Supreme Court Constitutional Decisions: The Case of Roosevelt's Court-Packing Plan," *International Review of Law and Economics* 12 (1992): 45–67;

Stephen R. Alton, "Loyal Lieutenant, Able Advocate: The Role of Robert H. Jackson in Franklin D. Roosevelt's Battle with the Supreme Court," *William and Mary Bill of Rights Journal* 5 (May 1997): 525–618; William E. Leuchtenburg, "When the People Spoke, What Did They Say? The Election of 1936 and the Ackerman Thesis," *Yale Law Journal* 108 (1999): 2077–2114; Jamie L. Carson and Benjamin A. Kleinerman, "A Switch in Time Saves Nine: Institutions, Strategic Actors, and FDR's Court-Packing Plan," *Public Choice* 113 (December 2002): 301–324; Daniel E. Ho and Kevin M. Quinn, "Did a Switch in Time Save Nine?" *Journal of Legal Analysis* 2 (Spring 2010): 69–113; Donovan Bisbee, "Driving the Three-Horse Team of Government: FDR's Judiciary Fireside Chat," *Rhetoric and Public Affairs* 3 (Fall 2018): 481–521; Warner W. Gardner, "Memories of the 1937 Constitutional Revolution, Part I," *Green Bag* 22 (Spring 2019): 219–233; and Alex Badas, "Policy Disagreement and Judicial Legitimacy: Evidence from the 1937 Court-Packing Plan," *Journal of Legal Studies* 48 (June 2019): 377–408. An account of FDR's decision not to use a constitutional amendment to address his problems with the Supreme Court is found in David E. Kyvig, "The Road Not Taken: FDR, the Supreme Court, and Constitutional Amendment," *Political Science Quarterly* 104 (1989): 463–481.

On court curbing in general, useful sources include Sidney Ratner, "Was the Supreme Court Packed by President Grant?" *Political Science Quarterly* 50 (September 1935): 343–358; Stuart S. Nagel, "Court-Curbing Periods in American History," *Vanderbilt Law Review* 18 (March 1965): 925–944; Gary L. McDowell, *Curbing the Courts: The Constitution and the Limits of Judicial Power* (Baton Rouge: Louisiana State University Press, 1988); Tom S. Clark, *The Limits of Judicial Independence* (New York: Cambridge University Press, 2011); and Joshua Braver, "Court-Packing: An American Tradition," *Boston College Law Review* 61 (2020): 2749–2808.

Although I write in the tradition of those authors who offer a political explanation for the Supreme Court's liberal "switch in time" in 1937, other scholars see more continuity than change in the justices' rulings. Among the leading works are Barry Cushman, *Rethinking the New Deal: The Structure of a Constitutional Revolution* (New York: Oxford University Press, 1998); G. Edward White, *The Constitution and the New Deal* (Cambridge, MA: Harvard University Press, 2000); and Richard

D. Friedman, "Switching Time and Other Thought Experiments: The Hughes Court and Constitutional Transformation," *University of Pennsylvania Law Review* 142 (June 1994): 1891–1984. Contrasting interpretations are the subject of Alan Brinkley, ed., "AHR Forum: The Debate over the Constitutional Revolution of 1937," *American Historical Review* 110 (October 2005): 1046–1115.

On Roosevelt's campaign to reorganize the executive branch, see Richard Polenberg, *Reorganizing Roosevelt's Government, 1936–1939: The Controversy over Executive Reorganization* (Cambridge, MA: Harvard University Press, 1966); Matthew J. Dickinson, *Bitter Harvest: FDR, Presidential Power and the Growth of the Presidential Branch* (New York: Cambridge University Press, 1997); and Barry Dean Karl, *Executive Reorganization and Reform in the New Deal* (Cambridge, MA: Harvard University Press, 1963). For near-contemporary accounts of the effort, see Louis Brownlow, *A Passion for Anonymity: The Autobiography of Louis Brownlow* (Chicago: University of Chicago Press, 1958); and Joseph P. Harris, "The Progress of Administrative Reorganization in the Seventy-Fifth Congress," *American Political Science Review* 21 (October 1937): 862–870. FDR's reorganization effort is also treated in Herbert Emmerich, *Federal Organization and Administrative Management* (University: University of Alabama Press, 1971); Peri E. Arnold, *Making the Managerial Presidency: Comprehensive Reorganization Planning, 1905–1980* (Princeton, NJ: Princeton University Press, 1986); John P. Burke, *The Institutional Presidency: Organizing and Managing the White House from FDR to Clinton*, 2nd ed. (Baltimore: Johns Hopkins University Press, 2000); and Richard E. Neustadt, "Presidency and Legislation: The Growth of Central Clearance," *American Political Science Review* 48 (September 1954): 641–671. On reorganization and other Roosevelt initiatives, an indispensable work is Sidney M. Milkis, *The President and the Parties: The Transformation of the American Party System since the New Deal* (New York: Oxford University Press, 1993).

Among biographies of Roosevelt, the most helpful concerning the matters covered in this book are three volumes by Kenneth S. Davis—*FDR: The Beckoning of Destiny, 1882–1928* (New York: Random House, 1971); *FDR: The New Deal Years, 1933–1937* (New York: Random House, 1979); and *FDR: Into the Storm, 1937–1940* (New York: Random House, 1993)—as well as Frank Freidel, *Franklin D. Roosevelt: A Rendezvous with Destiny* (Boston: Little, Brown, 1990); James MacGregor Burns, *Roosevelt: The Lion and the Fox, 1882–1940* (New York: Harcourt, 1956); Robert Dallek, *Franklin D. Roosevelt: A Political Life* (New York: Viking, 2017); Conrad Black, *Franklin Delano Roosevelt: Champion of Freedom* (New York: Public Affairs, 2003); Jean Edward Smith, *FDR* (New York: Random House, 2007); and William E. Leuchtenburg, *Franklin D. Roosevelt and the New Deal* (New York: Harper, 1963). Leuchtenburg also offers important insights into FDR's approach to the presidency in "The New Deal and the Analogue of War," in *Change and Continuity in Twentieth-Century America*, ed. John Braeman, Robert H. Bremner, and Everett Walters (Columbus: Ohio State University Press, 1964). Valuable oral history interviews of several administration figures, especially Samuel I. Rosenman and Robert H. Jackson, are available at the Columbia (University) Center for Oral History.

Other fine accounts of the Roosevelt presidency include Ira Katznelson, *Fear Itself: The New Deal and the Origins of Our Time* (New York: Liveright, 2013); and Alonzo L. Hamby, *For the Survival of Democracy: Franklin Roosevelt and the World Crisis of the 1930s* (New York: Free Press, 2004). Roosevelt's elections are thoroughly treated in Donald A. Ritchie, *Electing FDR: The New Deal Campaign of 1932* (Lawrence: University Press of Kansas, 2007); John W. Jeffries, *A Third Term for FDR: The Election of 1940* (Lawrence: University Press of Kansas, 2017); and Arthur M. Schlesinger Jr., *The Coming of the New Deal* (Boston: Houghton Mifflin, 1959), which covers the 1936 election and FDR's first term.

A number of memoirs by Roosevelt aides and associates are rich sources of insight and information. They include Harold Ickes, *The Secret Diary of Harold L. Ickes: The First Thousand Days, 1933–1936* (New York: Simon & Schuster, 1953), and *The Secret Diary of Harold L. Ickes: The Inside Struggle, 1936–1939* (New York: Simon & Schuster, 1954); Samuel I. Rosenman, *Working with Roosevelt* (New York: Harper & Brothers, 1952); James A. Farley, *Jim Farley's Story: The Roosevelt Years* (New York: McGraw-Hill, 1948); Frances Perkins, *The Roosevelt I Knew* (New York: Harper Colophon, 1964); Raymond Moley, *After Seven Years* (New York: Harper & Brothers, 1939); Robert H. Jackson, *That Man: An Insider's Portrait of Franklin D. Roosevelt*, ed. John Q. Barrett (New

York: Oxford University Press, 2003); Robert H. Jackson, *The Struggle for Judicial Supremacy: A Study of a Crisis in American Power* (New York: Knopf, 1941); Rexford G. Tugwell, *The Democratic Roosevelt* (Garden City, NY: Doubleday, 1957); Joseph P. Lash, *Dealers and Dreamers: A New Look at the New Deal* (New York: Doubleday, 1988); Carl Brent Swisher, ed., *Selected Papers of Homer Cummings: Attorney General of the United States, 1922–1939* (New York: Charles Scribner's Sons, 1939); Donald Richberg, *My Hero* (New York: G. P. Putnam's Sons, 1954); Max Freedman, ed., *Roosevelt and Frankfurter: Their Correspondence, 1928–1945* (Boston: Little, Brown, 1967); George Creel, *Rebel at Large: Recollections of Fifty Crowded Years* (New York: G. P. Putnam's Sons, 1947); and, although he was a leading antagonist in the court fight, Burton K. Wheeler, *Yankee from the West* (Garden City, NY: Doubleday, 1952).

On the Supreme Court in general, see Henry J. Abraham, *Justices, Presidents, and Senators: A History of Supreme Court Appointments from Washington to Clinton* (Lanham, MD: Rowman & Littlefield, 1999); William F. Swindler, *Court and Constitution in the 20th Century: The New Legality, 1932–1968* (Indianapolis: Bobbs-Merrill, 1970); Donald Greer Stephenson, *Campaigns and the Court: The U.S. Supreme Court in Presidential Elections* (New York: Columbia University Press, 1999); Barbara A. Perry, *The Priestly Tribe: The Supreme Court's Image in the American Mind* (Westport, CT: Praeger, 1999); Paul M. Collins Jr. and Matthew Eshbaugh-Soha, *The President and the Supreme Court: Going Public on Judicial Decisions from Washington to Trump* (New York: Cambridge University Press, 2019); David J. Garrow, "Mental Decrepitude on the U.S. Supreme Court," *University of Chicago Law Review* 67 (2000): 995–1087; Tara Grove, "The Origins (and Fragility) of Judicial Independence," *Vanderbilt Law Review* 71 (2018): 465–545; Robert Dahl, "Decision-Making in a Democracy: The Supreme Court as a National Policy-Maker," *Journal of Public Law* 6 (Fall 1957): 279–295; Richard Funston, "The Supreme Court and Critical Elections," *American Political Science Review* 69 (September 1975): 795–811; and John R. Schmidhauser, "The Justices of the Supreme Court: A Collective Portrait," *Midwest Journal of Political Science* 1 (February 1959): 1–57.

On the Supreme Court in this period, see C. Herman Pritchett, *The Roosevelt Court: A Study in Judicial Politics and Values, 1937–1947* (New

York: Macmillan, 1948); Peter H. Irons, *The New Deal Lawyers* (Princeton, NJ: Princeton University Press, 1982); Noah Feldman, *Scorpions: The Battles and Triumphs of FDR's Great Supreme Court Justices* (New York: Twelve, 2010); Merlo J. Pusey, *The Supreme Court Crisis* (New York: Macmillan, 1937); William G. Ross, *The Chief Justiceship of Charles Evans Hughes* (Columbia: University of South Carolina Press, 2007); Michael E. Parrish, *The Hughes Court; Justice, Rulings, and Legacy* (Santa Barbara, CA: ABC-CLIO, 2002); and Michael E. Parrish, "The Great Depression, the New Deal, and the American Legal Order," *Washington Law Review* 59 (1984): 723–740. Some biographies of justices are valuable as well, including Merlo J. Pusey, *Charles Evans Hughes*, vol. 2 (New York: Macmillan, 1951); Alpheus Thomas Mason, *Brandeis: A Free Man's Life* (New York: Viking, 1946); and Alpheus Thomas Mason, *Harlan Fiske Stone: Pillar of the Law* (New York: Viking, 1956). For insight into Hughes's chief justiceship, see Daniel J. Danelski, "The Influence of the Chief Justice in the Decisional Process of the Supreme Court," in *The Federal Judicial System: Readings in Process and Behavior*, ed. Thomas P. Jahnige and Sheldon Goldman (New York: Holt, Rinehart & Winston, 1968), 147–160. For a clerk's contemporary perspective on McReynolds, see Dennis J. Hutchinson and David J. Garrow, eds., *The Forgotten Memoir of John Knox: A Year in the Life of a Supreme Court Clerk in FDR's Washington* (Chicago: University of Chicago Press, 2002). An acerbic collective biography of the justices published on the eve of the court-packing effort is Drew Pearson and Robert Allen, *The Nine Old Men* (Garden City, NY: Doubleday, Doran, 1936).

On Congress in this period, see James T. Patterson, *Congressional Conservatism and the New Deal* (Lexington: University of Kentucky Press, 1967); Ronald L. Feinman, *The Twilight of Progressivism: The Western Republican Senators and the New Deal* (Baltimore: Johns Hopkins University Press, 1981); and James L. Sundquist, *The Decline and Resurgence of Congress* (Washington, DC: Brookings Institution, 1982). The Senate Judiciary Committee, "Reorganization of the Federal Judiciary: Adverse Report," June 14, 1937, is available at https://reason.com/wp-content/uploads/2020/10/Senate-Judiciary-Committee-Report-on-1937-Court-Packing-Legislation.pdf. An in-depth study of one senator's decision on court packing is Barry A. Crouch, "Dennis Chavez and Roosevelt's 'Court-Packing' Plan," *New Mexico Historical Review* 42 (1967): 261–280.

Public opinion polls from the 1930s are available in Hadley Cantril and Mildred Strunk, *Public Opinion, 1935–1946* (Princeton, NJ: Princeton University Press, 1951); and George H. Gallup, *The Gallup Poll: Public Opinion, 1935–1971*, vol. 1 (New York: Random House, 1972). Most of the presidential speeches and press conferences quoted in this volume, along with the text of many other documents, are available from the American Presidency Project website (https://www.presidency.ucsb.edu/people/president/franklin-d-roosevelt), the Miller Center at the University of Virginia (https://millercenter.org/president/fdroosevelt), or *The Public Papers and Addresses of Franklin D. Roosevelt* (https://quod.lib.umich.edu/p/ppotpus/4926313.1937.001?view=toc). A useful sample of mail received by FDR concerning court packing is presented in Lawrence W. Levine and Cornelia R. Levine, *The People and the President: America's Conversation with FDR* (Boston: Beacon Press, 2002).

INDEX